Advance Praise for EXIT is NOT a Four Letter Word

Passing on your financial advisory business *will happen*, and it will be *life-changing*. Buy, read, and re-read George Hartman's latest book *EXIT is NOT a Four Letter Word*. Otherwise, run the risk of wishing you had when it comes time for you to sell.

Ian R. Campbell, Author of *50 Hurdles: Business Transition Simplified*

Clear, concise, executable … George Hartman distills the essence of achieving succession preparedness and makes it easily digestible as we read the story of Henry, an advisor facing the universal succession choice points. The Coach's Recap crystalizes the takeaways in each chapter and the accompanying exercises give you a roadmap to construct your own transition plan. A must-have guide to start your succession strategy.

Mary Ann Buchanan, Founder & CEO, RIA Match

George has a unique ability to take difficult concepts and get to the heart of the matter. In a simple and straightforward style, he not only shares practical tactics that will help advisors increase the value of their businesses but also tackles some of the bigger, emotional issues that are tied up in succession. As importantly, it not only examines how to think about succession, but when.

Julie Littlechild, Founder, AbsoluteEngagement.com

I read a number of books on the subject of succession planning prior to my retirement and the sale after 40 years-of my share of our firm. Most dealt with valuation issues only. Today, were I to planning my retirement sometime in the near to intermediate future, George's latest book would have been invaluable to me as it covers a host of non-financial (but critical) matters — some of which I only learned were important AFTER I retired. I highly recommend *EXIT is NOT a Four Letter Word* as an excellent step-by-step guide to achieving a successful transition of your financial planning practice.

Jim Rogers, Founder, Rogers Group Financial, Past President MDRT

George Hartman has provided a simple yet elegant guide for financial advisors who are struggling with both succession of their business, and how and when to retire. He points out that few advisors have written succession plans and that many have never reflected on the important qualitative factors that can really drive business valuations. In my view, George's book is a must-read for any successful financial advisor — particularly those who have reached mid-career.

Greg Pollock, President & CEO, Advocis —— The Financial Advisors Association of Canada

George Hartman's great experience in succession and transition has proven to him that the most successful transition plans take years to develop and unfold. Through powerful stories that will motivate you to get started on your plan regardless of the type of advisory practice you have, George guides you through the steps to avoid the number one succession plan advisors have today — doing nothing. Get George's wisdom, his checklists and his plan — get this book!

Grant Hicks, National Director of Practice Management, Co-author, *"Guerrilla Marketing For Financial Advisors"*

Through a clear, story-telling format— featuring George Hartman (the coach) and Henry (his model client) — *EXIT is NOT a Four Letter Word* explores the steps, challenges and consequences of formulating a successful succession plan. Each chapter details their in-depth conversation, offers real-life examples, includes a Coach's Recap of the lesson plan and provides an exercise that allows readers to work through the process on their own. I could not put this fun-to-read book down. If you want to learn from one of the industry's most insightful coaches what it takes to realize the value of your life's work and proudly protect your legacy, neither should you.

Emily Chiang, CFP, Author, Selling Your Financial Advisory Practice

EXIT is NOT a Four Letter Word

Also by George Hartman

Risk is a Four-Letter Word: The Asset-Allocation Approach to Investing (1991)

Risk is STILL a Four-Letter Word (2001)

Blunder, Wonder, Thunder: Powering your Practice to New Heights (2010)

EXIT is NOT a Four Letter Word

How to Transition Your Advisory Practice —
Proudly and Profitably

George Hartman

Market Logics Inc., 43 Sunnydene Crescent, Toronto, ON Canada M4N 3J5
416-489-4848 • www.marketlogics.ca

Market Logics

Intelligence-Based Solutions

Publisher: Market Logics Inc.

Editor: Jefferson Orlando

Design: Karen Marren Design Inc.

Photographer: Norm Betts

Print Production: Marquis Book Publishers

ISBN – 978-0-9813744-1-3

Printed and Bound in Canada

To my son, Jack

— you came into my life at a time I did not expect and, in fact, did not think I deserved. You brought joy, hope, and love such as I have never experienced.

I marvel at what you have learned in such a short time. I marvel even more at what you have taught. Thank you for allowing me to see the world through the eyes of a beautiful five-year-old. It is a far better place now that you are in it.

Acknowledgements

If it takes a village to raise a child, it certainly takes a council of elders to produce a book.

My sincere gratitude goes to the legion of researchers, writers, and commentators whose wisdom regarding succession planning helped shape my own thinking on the subject. Many of their publications are listed in the "Recommended Reading" pages near the end of this book.

I am indebted to the thousands of financial advisors with whom I have worked over the past 40 years. Through their real-life experiences, they have taught me how to separate what is real from what is conceptual.

I am grateful to the many conference organizers who have given me a stage from which to express my thoughts and theories and dialogue with audiences across the globe.

To my friends at *Investment Executive*, thank you for allowing me to communicate and interact with financial advisors across the country and around the world through more than ten years of writing my monthly *Coach's Forum* column. Special mention goes to Grant McIntyre, Senior Editor, for his ongoing support and passion for distributing sound practice management advice to the financial advisor community.

As she did with my last book, Karen Marren's creative cover design cleverly conveys the essence of what this book is all about the moment you see it. Norm Betts' photographic trickery coupled with Jeffery Orlando's editing talent make me look and sound better than I deserve.

At a personal level, my most heartfelt thanks go to my wife, Julie. Without her steadfast encouragement and extraordinary effort, this book would still be an ambition. I am truly blessed to have such a beautiful, loving cheerleader and best friend!

Finally, to my son, Jack, thank you so much for inspiring me with your soaring spirit, unconditional love, and never-ending curiosity. You have brought an unbelievable joy to my life. This book is dedicated to you.

Foreword

The impending succession crisis in the financial services industry is not without its own peculiar irony. How is it that the vast majority of aging advisors, who are skillfully guiding the financial fortunes of millions of aging clients, are themselves without succession plans?

A reasonable explanation is that experts have always struggled with seeking help, especially in their own area of expertise. In the same way that doctors often make terrible patients, advisors continue to have a hard time exiting their businesses and monetizing one of their largest assets to secure their own retirements. But every profession gives rise to the internal sector expert — the doctor's doctor, the lawyer's lawyer. This important book cements George Hartman's reputation as the advisor's advisor.

Coaching advisors on their succession plans is complex. Few do it well. This aspect of practice management is fraught with emotion, fear, anxiety and equivocation. It has always required one part finance and one part Freud. The perception remains that exit planning is a bit painful. The stories of wildly successful advisors who have achieved great financial success exiting their practices often go unreported because of the confidentiality clauses in their sales agreements. Failed exits, on the other hand, are reported frequently and discussed broadly in an industry whose chattering leads most to believe exit planning is, and always has been, a waste of time.

EXIT is NOT a Four Letter Word will change that narrative. This book has the potential to change the financial fortunes of advisors who implement a refreshing new exit process, delivered here in an entertaining and informative style. The broader financial services industry will benefit from advisors who put an end to the chaos caused by practitioners who only know how to "grow", but not how to "go."

The exit planning process described in this book isn't just about unlocking more value at the end of a long, distinguished career; it's about building more valuable and intrinsically more rewarding practices today. Advisors who can articulate to their clients — especially business owner clients — their own struggles with succession planning present themselves as authentic and accessible. They possess a hard-earned wisdom that is almost always rewarded by clients who hand over their own sale proceeds to be invested.

This book is not a remix of old familiar ideas on a subject as old as business itself. This is a book of firsts. In much the same way that The E-Myth redefined what it means to be an entrepreneur and *Good to Great* changed our understanding of leadership, *EXIT is NOT a Four Letter Word* will change the meaning of "exit." "Hope" is a four-letter word, as is "help." This extraordinary book offers both.

If you are an advisor who wants to exit in the next ten years, start now by purchasing a copy of this book. It will be one of the smartest financial decisions you make to protect your life's work.

If you are a supplier to financial advisors, buy this book by the truckload and support advisors where they need help the most. When succession planning goes well for an advisor — when they find their exit before the end finds them — it is you who will be rewarded for your wisdom and foresight. The alternative is to keep giving away golf balls and watching an industry help everyone but itself.

Tom Deans, Ph.D.
Author of *Every Family's Business* and *Willing Wisdom*

Contents

Introduction 1

Chapter 1
Why plan? 5
Another Illustrative Case in Point 15
Coach's Recap. 18
My Succession Plan 20

Chapter 2
Where is the money?. 23
Another Illustrative Case in Point 31
Coach's Recap. 34
My Succession Plan 36

Chapter 3
What is my practice worth? 37
Another Illustrative Case in Point 45
Coach's Recap. 47
My Succession Plan 49

Chapter 4
How do I prepare myself?. 51
Another Illustrative Case in Point 61
Coach's Recap. 63
My Succession Plan 65

Chapter 5
When is the right time?. 67
Another Illustrative Case in Point 78
Coach's Recap. 80
My Succession Plan 82

Chapter 6
What is the best exit option?. 83
Another Illustrative Case in Point 93
Coach's Recap. 95
My Succession Plan 98

Chapter 7

Which exit option is for me?. 99

Another Illustrative Case in Point 109

Coach's Recap. 111

My Succession Plan 112

Chapter 8

Who should be my successor? 113

Another Illustrative Case in Point 123

Coach's Recap. 125

My Succession Plan 127

Chapter 9

What about family as successor? 129

Another Illustrative Case in Point 141

Coach's Recap. 143

My Succession Plan 144

Chapter 10

How do I set myself up for success?. 145

Another Illustrative Case in Point 158

Coach's Recap. 160

My Succession Plan 161

Chapter 11

How do I make it happen? 165

Another Illustrative Case in Point 174

Coach's Recap. 177

My Succession Plan 179

Epilogue 181

Index 184

Recommended Reading 185

About George Hartman 186

Speaking, Coaching & Consulting. 187

Speaking. 187

Coaching 187

Consulting 188

"The Chinese use two brush strokes to write the word 'crisis.'
One brush stroke stands for danger; the other for opportunity.
In a crisis, be aware of the danger—but recognize the opportunity.
John F. Kennedy

Introduction

This book is the modest attempt by a concerned observer to alert the financial services industry to a looming crisis and to motivate the only people who can do anything about it to act. The crisis is the aging of financial advisors. The people with the solution are those same advisors. The action is succession planning.

We have all heard the warnings — the average age of advisors is mid-to-late fifties; half of the advisor population will reach retirement age within the next ten years; only one in ten advisors has a written succession plan; there are an insufficient number of new advisors to replace those who will die, become disabled, or retire.

Yet it is only in the past ten years that we have really even begun to acknowledge the issues. Up until then, financial advisory practices either faded away with their founders or had their clients scattered among other advisors who may or may not have wanted to accept them. That was not so great for an industry that stakes its value proposition on helping people plan for and manage their future well-being.

Today, large, well-run, high-profile practices trade hands among like-minded advisors for millions of dollars. I am not worried about them. My concern is with the hundreds of thousands of advisors who have the majority of their personal wealth tied up in their small-to-medium sized practices. Moreover, they are counting on those businesses to fund their own retirement lifestyle.

Many will be tragically disappointed because they waited too long, planned too little, and assumed too much. But it doesn't have to be that way. The process of transitioning a financial advisory practice from one advisor to another is relatively straightforward and follows the same path advisors use to counsel clients — create a vision for the future, conduct a reality check on the situation today, and draw a map to take you from where you are to where you want to go.

So if the warnings about the need to act are there and the process is familiar, why do 90% of advisors not have a plan?

In Chapter 1, I talk about the "terrible toos" — I'm *too* young, it's *too* soon, it's *too* much work, I'm *too* important to my business. I hear these excuses all the time; however, I think the real reason for their procrastination is that many advisors have come to believe that succession planning somehow signals the end of their career. In fact, it should be the beginning of the last and greatest phase of their business and the birth of their legacy.

I have been coaching financial advisors for more than 25 years, and they have taught me a lot. In addition to all the practice management insights, one of the most valuable lessons I have learned is that, given sound reasoning and a logical methodology, serious financial advisors will make a focused effort to change their habits and their businesses for the better.

So that is what this book attempts to do — provide the rationale and the routine to motivate you to prepare for the eventual transition of your business to the most qualified successor. The result will be continued service to clients who trust you, greater value to you for your life's work, and greater certainty about the industry's future.

Succession planning is not an event — it is a journey. To help us along the way, I have re-introduced Henry, the central character from my book *Blunder, Wonder, Thunder — Powering Your Practice to New Heights.* We first worked with Henry a number of years ago when his practice had reached a plateau. Having broken through that ceiling and built his business to an enviable position, we will now follow Henry through various coaching conversations with me as he writes and directs the final act in the story of his life's work.

Henry is not a real-life advisor; he is an amalgam of many with whom I have worked. However, all the conversations played out in this book have actually happened in coaching sessions with hundreds of advisors.

I will also readily admit that not all of the ideas expressed are original. I have been a "student of the business" for four decades and have assimilated many of the best ideas I have heard or read into my writings and presentations so often that I have come to think of them as my own. I offer my thanks, therefore, to the great minds who created this wisdom and apologize if I have borrowed it inappropriately or misinterpreted what was intended.

One resource in particular I would like to mention is the first book I ever read on the subject of succession planning for entrepreneurs, long before it was such a popular topic. Published in 2008, *Exiting Your Business, Protecting Your Wealth by John Leonetti*[1] was instrumental in piquing my interest and shaping my ideas. You will see some of John's insights reflected here and I highly recommend his book as the definitive textbook in this field.

The truth of the matter is that you will leave your business someday. The question is, will you be in control of your exit, or will you allow fate and circumstance to dictate what happens to the business you have spent so much of your life building?

Come join Henry and me. I think you will enjoy the journey!

---

1   www.pinnacleequitysolutions.com

Wisdom begins in wonder."
Socrates

Chapter 1

Why plan?

"Well, Henry," I said, "that's it for another year — unless, of course, you are planning one of your Florida golf trips this winter."

Henry, a well-established and successful financial advisor, and I were sitting on the patio at the golf club where we were both members. It was the final day before the course shut down for the season, and the cold wind that buffeted the flagstick on the nearby 18th green was testing our resolve to have one last outdoor post-round beer.

"Actually," Henry said, "I have a week scheduled in January to visit my older brother near Phoenix. He and his wife retired there about five years ago. They have a nice house right on a golf course, and the last time I was there, we played at least nine holes every day. It was great!"

"Sounds idyllic — do they enjoy living in Arizona?" I asked.

"Yes and no," he replied thoughtfully. "They certainly don't miss the northern winters, but are they enjoying retirement as much as they'd hoped? I don't think so. My brother built and ran a very successful plumbing supply business, which he sold to a couple of his employees when he retired. Because I manage his portfolio, I know how much he got from the sale. He doesn't have to worry financially; however, I'm not sure that he is as well-off emotionally. It's not that he is unhappy — but the spark that he used to have when he was working seems to be missing. Does that make sense?"

"It sure does," I responded. "It is not at all uncommon for entrepreneurs who sell their businesses to feel they have lost a big chunk of their lives. Whether it's losing contact with staff and customers, feeling unimportant because no one is looking to them for guidance or decision-making, or just plain missing "the action," leaving behind their life's work can take a heavy toll on some people. Sure, having money helps, but unless it is being spent on a lifestyle that provides as much satisfaction as the work did, there is often going to be a hole in one's psyche."

"Spoken like a true coach!" Henry mocked.

"Can't help that," I laughed. "I *am* a coach and I must be a pretty good one to have helped someone as ornery as you get your business to where it is today! My, my, how attitudes change! When you and I first started working together — what is it now, six years ago? — you were so respectful and polite. Now your practice is three times as large, you make five times as much money, and you are ten times as cocky! I'm not so sure I like what I've created!"

We both laughed. Just then, a huge gust of wind blew some of the same leaves that had hidden my ball in the fairway on #18 onto the patio and around our legs.

"It's time to go inside," I suggested. "Perhaps another beer?"

"I think we should have something to eat instead," Henry proposed. "Losing your ball on the last hole cost you the match, so I'll take my winnings in the form of dinner, if you don't mind?"

"No, I don't mind at all," I countered, "because I'm pretty sure I'm still well ahead overall this season! Besides, it will also give us a chance to have a bit of a serious discussion about the next phase in your career."

"And just what's that?" Henry demanded, suddenly turning a bit crusty.

"*Your* retirement," I replied with emphasis.

"Augh," Henry reacted snappishly, "there's nothing to talk about there. I have no plan to retire."

"That's exactly what we need to talk about then — your *lack* of a plan," I said as we headed for the door to the dining room.

The dining room was quiet with only a few other late-season stalwarts seated well away from us. The waiter rattled off the daily special and then left us with menus.

"I think you may have spoiled my appetite," Henry began sternly, "with talk about my retirement. I'm too young to even be thinking that way."

"Actually, Henry, I wasn't suggesting that you were ready to retire," I said, defending myself. "I said we needed to talk about you not having a plan for the day when you ultimately *do* decide to transition out of your business. How many of your clients around your age would you let get away with not having a retirement plan in place, even if they don't intend to actually quit work for years?"

"That's different," Henry replied. "That's my job — people come to me to help them take control of their finances and create a plan that will give them the best chance of meeting their objectives, regardless of their stage in life. If they happen to be at the age where retirement planning should be part of it, that's what we do."

"And at approximately what age do you encourage your clients to get serious about their retirement plan?" I probed.

"It's more about their intended retirement date than their age," he answered, "and the lifestyle they want in retirement. Some plans take longer to achieve clients' objectives than others. Ten, fifteen, even twenty years wouldn't be uncommon."

"And what do you think *I* do, Henry?" I asked.

"You help advisors gain control of their businesses so they can achieve…" Henry's voice trailed off as he quickly recognized the parallel.

"OK, OK," Henry reluctantly admitted, "I get what you're saying. However, my situation *is* different. I am not sure I will ever retire. I love what I do; I enjoy my clients; I can pretty much decide how hard I work; and I make a darn good living. Why would I want to retire?"

"Well, the truth is that you *will* leave your business one day," I countered. "The question is, will *you* be in control of how you exit? Or will fate and circumstance dictate what happens to the business that you have spent your life building?"

Just then, the waiter returned. We quickly looked at the menus, and he took our dinner orders.

Henry was quiet for a few minutes until he finally said, only half-jokingly, "You know I really don't like you as much when you state the obvious and it makes me look foolish."

"I'm not too concerned about that," I retorted with a chuckle. "Remember how you balked at some of the things I suggested the last time we did serious work together? We don't have to agree on everything. In fact, it's healthy if we thoughtfully challenge each other's thinking from time to time. The good news for you is that, at the end of the day, it's your life and you get to make choices about how you are going to live it.

"Nonetheless, as your long-time and, I assume, still-in-good-standing coach, my role is to help you analyze your business from time to time and bring important issues to your attention, along with ideas on how others in similar situations have dealt with them. In this instance, knowing what I know about you and your practice, it's time for us to create a written plan that puts you in control of your transition or exit from the business regardless of how or when that happens. I can't be any more straightforward. Does that make sense to you?"

Henry was still unenthusiastic. "I know a lot of advisors my age, and I don't hear many of them talking about their succession plans," he said.

"That doesn't surprise me at all," I responded. "Research shows that only about 10% of advisors actually have a written exit plan. I can also tell you that two out of every three of my coaching assignments these days involve some element of succession planning. It's one of the hottest topics in the industry."

"Why the sudden interest," Henry asked. "Coaches run out of things to talk about?"

I ignored his sarcasm. "It's a matter of simple demographics. Like the rest of us, many financial advisors are aging baby boomers who are finally starting to realize they are not immortal or that they want to have a life beyond their career."

"Humph!" Henry snorted again.

"Let me ask you, Henry, do you have a relatively recent will — a document that describes what will happen to your assets when you die?"

"Of course," he answered. "I wouldn't be much of an advisor if I didn't follow the same advice I give my clients about having an up-to-date will, would I?"

"I think you might be surprised to know how many advisors do *not* follow their own advice in this area," I suggested, "but let's not get into that. I assume, however, that you also have a 'living will' or Powers of Attorney that dictate how your personal assets and your life will be managed in the event you are not able to make decisions on your own?"

"Certainly!" said Henry, reacting as if I should not have even asked the question.

"Well," I continued, "a succession plan is like a will or power of attorney for your business, with one major difference. It also describes what will happen when *you* decide you want to make some major changes in your life.

"You've had your practice for a long time, right?" I asked.

"Just celebrated 25 years about six months ago," Henry replied, justifiably proud.

"That's wonderful," I congratulated him. "So you've spend a good part of your life building your business."

"It's hard to believe it's been 25 years," Henry said, "but it hasn't really felt like work. Sure there were tough times, but I've really enjoyed the ride."

"Good on you for seeing the big picture," I offered. "Now, you and I both know that practices such as yours are commanding big bucks today from people looking to buy solid books of business. You do not have to give me details of your personal financial position, but I am guessing that your practice is a significant part of your personal wealth. And that is possibly going to be important — either to augment your eventual retirement income or as a value to be passed on to your family."

"I haven't really thought much about it," Henry responded, not very convincingly.

"Of course you have!" I challenged him. "You've seen other advisors your age leave the business, and you have some idea of how much they got for their books. I am willing to bet you have also received offers yourself that, while you may have dismissed them at the time, got you thinking about the value you had built in your practice. Right?"

"I actually can't believe the numbers that are being thrown around," Henry admitted. "Knowing the quality of the books of business that were sold, if the dollars I am hearing about are even close to accurate, my practice has to be worth a lot more than I ever imagined it would be. Wasn't that one of the objectives of the work we did together anyway?"

"Nice of you to remember!" I joked. "But I also know from that experience that money isn't your primary motivator — you also care deeply about your clients."

"Without them, I don't have a business," Henry said. "Besides which, I like to think many of them are more than just clients — they're friends."

"I'm sure they feel the same way, Henry," I suggested. "So let me summarize, if I may. You have spent a lifetime building your business to the point where it is one of your most valuable financial assets, if not *the* most valuable. You expect it to help fund your retirement or your estate. On top of that, because of the deep personal relationships you have with your clients, you feel an obligation to ensure they always receive the best advice and service possible. Is that a fair summation?"

"Yes, it is," Henry reluctantly agreed, seeming to sense there was more to come.

"Then, Henry," I said more seriously, "I can't imagine why you wouldn't want to be in control of what happens to you and your business when you ultimately exit from it — voluntarily or otherwise. Why you would not want to decide who carries on your work with your clients. And, very important, what you want your legacy to be.

"When I was young in my career, working in a large financial institution, I was very fortunate to have a great personal mentor. Among the many nuggets of great advice he gave me is one that has always stood out for me. He said, "The true value of your work here won't really be known until two years after you're gone." Despite your many years in the industry, it is the state in which you leave things when you are no longer around that will ultimately determine how you are remembered.

"How do you want to be remembered, Henry?"

At that point, the waiter arrived with our meals, and our conversation fell to less serious matters as we ate.

———————————

By the time coffee and dessert came, I could tell by the distant look and increasingly long periods of silence that Henry was thinking about our discussion, so I took the opportunity to bring us back to the topic of his succession plan.

"You know, Henry," I began, "you're not the only advisor with whom I have had this type of conversation — about the need for them to think seriously about their exit strategy. Recall that nine out of ten advisors do not have a written plan in place. There are lots of reasons for that."

"Oh yeah," he replied, "What are their excuses? Maybe I can borrow one."

"Well, I believe one reason is that many advisors feel that having a succession plan somehow marks the beginning of the end of their careers. It's almost like the fear some people have of discussing life insurance or their wills — as if just thinking about it will hasten their death.

"The truth, however, is that succession isn't an event — it's a process. Very few advisors circle a date on the calendar and, at 5:00 PM on that day, hand in their keys to the office and are gone. Most succession plans anticipate a gradual *transition* rather than an abrupt *exit*. The unfortunate thing is that, for lots of people, succession has become synonymous with 'selling your business,' and the thought of that frightens most entrepreneurs, including financial advisors. Exit, in fact, has become a four-letter word for many."

"I don't think I'd use profanity to describe it," Henry protested. "I just haven't gotten around to planning for it. I'm too busy and, besides, as I said earlier, I'm too young to worry about retirement."

"Ah, the 'terrible toos,'" I jumped in. "I'm *too* busy; I'm *too* important; it's *too* soon; I'm *too* attached; it's *too* complicated; and the most common one I hear, to do what? I've heard all of these from advisors who have no idea how they'd spend their time without their business to go to every day.

"I know some advisors also fear their clients and support staff will react negatively if they learn the advisor they are counting on either for advice or employment is contemplating his or her own retirement. The truth on that one, however, is that they are likely already worried because they don't know what's going on inside the advisor's head. Both clients and staff would feel a lot less vulnerable if they knew there was a plan in place to ensure their ongoing financial security.

"Then there are those advisors who are considering one of their children as successor. They will postpone their planning out of concern about sibling rivalry — if one child is brought into the business and others are not.

"Wanting to avoid these types of conflicts can drive an advisor to put off their plan until it gets to crunch time for a decision and circumstances force their hand. Not a great way to deal with such an important issue, in my view."

"Ok, I'll concede that some advisors need to get to work on their transition plan, as you call it, sooner than others," Henry relented. "However, as you pointed out yourself, I've received a number of offers to buy my business — some of them quite attractive. I *do* appreciate that the work we did together put my practice on solid footing, made it easier to manage and grow, and definitely increased its value. But if I have other advisors knocking on my door all the time to buy my business, how much planning do I really have to do?"

"Well, thanks for acknowledging that we did some good!" I chuckled. "And you are absolutely correct — it's a seller's market these days, and there are lots of people around who'd buy a great practice like yours in a heartbeat. However, the big question is, would you sell your business to *just anybody*?

"I'm not even going to make you answer that because I know you wouldn't. You would want someone who you felt would extend the same level of care and service to your clients as you do. Ideally, they would share a passion for financial planning and use an investment approach similar to your own so clients' portfolios and insurance programs are not all 'undone' and re-jigged. You would want your team to be treated fairly and respected for the work they do. Recall what I said earlier too about your legacy. What would you look for in the person who is going to be the custodian of your legacy? Yes, there are lots of buyers out there — most of them, however, you wouldn't want to sell to."

"Even so," Henry continued stubbornly, "I am at least five years away from retiring — more likely ten. Do I really need to start a formal plan now?"

"In my experience," I answered, "the best transition plans evolve over a five- to ten-year period. There is much to be done. First and foremost, we will want to make the business more *saleable*. That might seem like an odd comment, given what a great practice you have today and the current bull market for books of business. The reality, however, is that your business is set up to work for you. You have systems and processes that you designed, technology that you put in place, and customized approaches that fit your philosophies and way of doing business. In other words, you have tailor-made your practice to work for you. But will your way work for everyone? Perhaps for many, but to the extent you can make your business adaptable to the needs of a potential buyer, the more attractive it will be. It can easily take a couple of years to put things in place to make your business more saleable and, hence, more valuable.

"Similarly, you'll want to make the business *scalable*. You have exceeded the size of business you aspired to when we undertook our last assignment. At that time, you didn't feel the need to build a practice to the sky, so to speak, because you wanted time for other things, like golf and travel. By my observation, you have more than accomplished what you set out to do."

"I do have it pretty good right now," Henry admitted.

"Yes, you do," I agreed. "However, you'll want to be able to demonstrate that, with the right management, your business can grow even bigger than what you've created. That means having marketing, sales, and service systems in place that can be leveraged for growth.

"I think I can handle all of that," Henry proclaimed, "and I don't think it will take years!"

"Perhaps not," I replied, "if that were all you had to do. However, you still have a business to run, and now, on top of the daily demands of that and these other tasks I have just described, you also have to find, negotiate with, and integrate the right successor.

"What do they look like? What skills and experience do they need? Where do you find them? How do you approach them? What kind of a deal do you want? Once identified, how do you integrate them? How do you introduce them to your clients so they are reassured and stick with the new advisor? What if, after a period of time, it turns out that your first choice in successor is just not a 'good fit' and you have to start over?

"Frankly, Henry, trying to do all this well in a couple of years can be daunting and seldom gets the best results. The process will begin to control you, rather than the other way around. Is that the kind of pressure you want when you have been so successful in reducing the stress of managing a vibrant business?"

Henry sat quietly thinking for a full minute until he said, "So what's involved?"

"Similar to last time, Henry. You know my mantra — *standardized process; customized solution*. I have a disciplined process that we will walk through to make sure we touch all the bases and consider all aspects of a successful transition. By the end of it, we will have a plan that describes the why, when, how, and who of your transition and puts you in control.

"The plan won't be chiselled in stone — you can change things as experience or new insights dictate. The important thing is that you will have a frame of reference for making decisions and a guide for you and others who will be part of the process to follow. Does that make sense to you?"

It took another minute or so until Henry finally said, "OK, I'm in. I assume your normal fee applies?"

"Actually, my fees have gone up since our last engagement — supply and demand, you know!" I laughed. "But don't worry; you get our 'preferred client pricing' because I like you so much! I will call you tomorrow when we both have our calendars in front of us, and we can plan our first formal session. In the meantime, it is both my personal and professional pleasure to buy you dinner!"

•

Another Illustrative Case in Point

The Long Goodbye

Bob had built a great business over a 20-year period. In fact, many industry insiders looked upon him as a 'poster boy' for how a practice should be run.

At the age of 55, Bob became very attracted to a new business opportunity in another part of the country. While he certainly enjoyed his work as an advisor and wasn't looking for a change, he felt his practice pretty much ran on autopilot, and he was no longer motivated by the thought of doing the same thing for the next 20 years. The chance to "build something all over" was exciting and stimulated him.

After long deliberation and consultation with his family, Bob made the decision to sell his business while he was still young enough to pursue his new opportunity with the same energy he had employed in building his financial advisory practice.

He had a formal valuation of the business completed, which indicated that a $1.8 million price tag was not out of line. By Bob's calculations, a down payment of $1 million with the balance paid over two years would provide the capital to both launch the new business and maintain his lifestyle through two to three years of start-up.

With that valuation in hand, Bob quietly let it be known in the industry that he was open to offers. Not surprisingly, the reaction was swift, with half a dozen suitors immediately expressing interest. After all, this was one of the industry's most respected practices coming on the market.

However, what followed was typical:

- A number of the first suitors turned out to be "tire-kickers," more interested in comparing their own businesses with Bob's than actually buying.

- Most did not have the financial capacity to meet Bob's price or terms.

- None matched the profile Bob had in his mind for his successor in terms of experience, philosophy, and approach to managing a practice.

- The due-diligence process was extremely frustrating, with multiple non-disclosure agreements, exchanges of information, 'lock-up' periods and high-level discussions.

After more than nine months of distraction and effort, Bob was no closer to finding a successor. Shortly after, one of the industry's leading 'consolidator' firms contacted Bob. They were on an ambitious acquisition campaign and had heard of his interest in selling. Even though they never said so, they were obviously also aware that he had not been able to find a buyer to his liking. Over a very expensive dinner in a hard-to-get-into restaurant, they offered Bob an all-cash payment of $1.4 million if he would agree to sell within 90 days. Their plan was to merge Bob's office with another they had in the community.

At first, Bob thought the quick sale and upfront cash were attractive, even though the total price was less than he was seeking. Still, he worried about:

- Getting overall fair value for his life's work

- Having a secure income for the next two years

- How clients would be served under a new dealer firm and management

- Whether his staff would be retained and how they'd be treated

- How his "legacy" — the business he'd built — would be run

Bob rejected the offer, confident he could find a more suitable successor.

About six weeks later, while attending a conference, Bob was telling another advisor in his dealer firm about his efforts to find the right buyer for his practice. The other advisor immediately indicated that he had been looking to expand outside his community, which was less than an hour's drive from where Bob's practice was located. Perhaps they should talk more seriously. Bob had great respect for the other advisor, so he jumped at the chance, and a follow-up meeting was scheduled.

Two months later, Bob and his associate had completed their mutual due diligence, and a Letter of Intent was signed. The financial terms were in line with Bob's expectations; however, the agreement also called for Bob to stay on through a 12-month transition period. During that time, in addition to continuing to serve his clients, he was to assess the systems at the other office to determine if the same efficiencies Bob's office enjoyed could be replicated. There would also be a formal plan to announce Bob's retirement to his clients and staff and to transition ownership, management, and client relationships to the new owner.

The transaction was formalized in an Agreement of Purchase and Sale, which took each party's independent legal counsel about a month to put together. Similarly, since the purchaser was partly using borrowed funds to meet the down payment requirements, his lending institution required several weeks to complete their underwriting of his loan.

By the time the Agreement was effective, almost a year and a half had passed since Bob first contemplated selling his business. Add to that the 12-month transition period, and what started out looking like a simple and easy succession took two and a half years to initiate, with another two years to complete the buyout — almost five years in total before Bob was completely clear of his advisory practice.

Coach's Recap

- You have likely spent much of your working life building your business to the point where it is one of your most valuable financial assets, if not *the* most valuable. You expect it to help fund your retirement or your estate. On top of that, because of the deep personal relationships you have with your clients, you feel an obligation to ensure they always receive the best advice and service possible.

- The day will inevitably come when you *will* leave your business — voluntarily or otherwise. The question is, will *you* be in control of how you exit? Or will fate and circumstance dictate what happens to the business that you have spent your lifetime building?

- Only about 10% of advisors actually have a written exit plan. Approximately another 40% have *thought* about their exit strategy but have not committed anything to writing. That leaves half of advisors with no plan whatsoever.

- Advisors more often postpone their succession plan for emotional reasons than financial, such as:
  - I'm too young to retire
  - It's too soon to plan
  - I'm too important to the business
  - I'm too attached to my business
  - It's too much work
  - It's too complicated
  - I'm too busy
  - I have no idea what else I would do

- Many financial advisors feel they will be giving up a big part of "who they are" when they sell their businesses. Whether it's loss of contact with staff and clients, feeling unimportant because they are no longer making decisions for the business, or just plain missing "the action." the thought of leaving behind their life's work can weigh heavily on their emotions.

- Some advisors feel that planning their succession somehow marks the beginning of the end of their careers. The truth, however, is that succession is not an event — it is a process. Most succession plans anticipate a gradual *transition* rather than an abrupt *exit*.

- Transitioning from your business takes time — likely more than you expect. You need to:
  - Make your business saleable
  - Make your business scalable
  - Make your business transferable
  - Find, negotiate with, and integrate your successor
  - Reassure clients and staff so they stay after the transition

- The most successful transition plans take five to ten years to develop and unfold.

My Succession Plan

Exercise #1 – Why plan?

Assess your current position with respect to succession planning by answering the following questions:

1. **My transition/succession plan is:** (Check most applicable)
   - ☐ Written down and up-to-date
   - ☐ Written down; requires updating
   - ☐ In my head and up-to-date
   - ☐ In my head; requires updating
   - ☐ Something I wish I had
   - ☐ Something I don't need

2. **I think a transition/succession plan should help me:**
   (Check all that apply)
   - ☐ Take control of my eventual exit from the business
   - ☐ Maximize the value when I exit/transition
   - ☐ Ensure I can fund my own retirement
   - ☐ Give my family, clients and staff confidence and peace of mind
   - ☐ Ensure my legacy is what I want it to be
   - ☐ Actually, I don't need a transition/succession plan

3. **I do not have a written transition/succession plan because I am:**
   (Check all that apply)
   - ☐ Too busy
   - ☐ Too young
   - ☐ Too important to my business
   - ☐ Too attached to my business
   - ☐ Unsure what I would do after
   - ☐ Concerned clients and staff will react negatively
   - ☐ Concerned about conflict among potential successors
   - ☐ Not sure how to develop a plan
   - ☐ Not concerned about selling my business at a good price when I am ready
   - ☐ Actually, I have a written succession plan that gives me confidence

4. **Things that might motivate me to consider selling my practice are:**
   (Check all that apply)

   ☐   Opportunity to cash in at a good price

   ☐   Tired of the business

   ☐   Want to mentor someone else

   ☐   Want different lifestyle e.g. more travel, hobbies, etc.

   ☐   Health concerns

   ☐   Family issues e.g. caregiver, divorce, death of spouse, etc.

   ☐   Other (Specify) _____

5. **Would I buy my own practice right now?**   ☐ Yes   ☐ No

   Why? _____

   _____   _____

6. **To whom:**

   a. <u>Could</u> I sell my practice today? (Name) _____

   Why? _____

   b. <u>Would</u> I sell my practice today?   ☐ Yes   ☐ No

   Why?_____

7. **My priority interest is:**

   ☐   What happens to the business after I am gone

   ☐   What happens to me after the business is gone

   ☐   Finding the right balance

   ☐   Other (Specify) _____

8. **My targeted transition/succession timeframe is:**

   ☐ Less than 2 years   ☐ 3-5 years   ☐ 5-10 years   ☐ 10+ years

"Entrepreneurship is living a few years of your life like most people won't... so you can spend the rest of your life like most people can't."
Warren Tracy

Chapter 2

Where is the money?

It took a couple of weeks to match our schedules before Henry and I were sitting in his boardroom to begin our formal work on his transition plan. After the small talk, I started the real conversation by expressing my congratulations and appreciation.

"First off, Henry, I want to commend you for committing to this project. I know you were more than a little reluctant when we first talked about the need for you to have a definitive succession plan. Perhaps, even now, you are not fully convinced of the value of this process, but I want to assure you that, like many tasks in life, the hardest part is getting started. Once we are underway, I am very confident that you'll not only see the value, you will become excited by the possibilities and choices you have regarding your business."

"Actually, I have no doubt there is value in the process," Henry countered, "but I confess to still being somewhat skeptical as to whether it is of value to *me* at this time in my career."

"In that case, then, I thank you for trusting me," I said.

"Oh, I trust you — and probably more so here than on the golf course. I think I may have seen a foot wedge or two out there this year," Henry teased.

"I won't even dignify that comment with a response," I poked right back.

"Instead, let me begin with a 'big picture' perspective on a couple of key concepts that might ease your mind by helping you see how very much in control you actually are when it comes to decisions around your own exit strategy, including its timing.

"In my experience, there are two major dimensions of your life that have to align before we can say you are ready to retire or transition out of your practice. The first is your *financial capacity*, and the second is your *emotional enthusiasm.*

"For a transition to be truly successful, you have to score well on both measures. Being financially able, but not emotionally enthusiastic, sounds a bit like the story you told me about your brother retiring to Arizona — long on money — short on enthusiasm. On the other hand, being emotionally charged about retirement without the means to enjoy it can be frustrating and demoralizing.

"The good news for you is that, in both cases, you get to decide on the benchmark; for example, what amount of financial resources would you want to have to consider yourself financially able to retire? And on the emotional side, you are the only one who can say yes or no to being excited about making such a major change in your life.

"Based on our last conversation, I am guessing that, at this stage in your life, you are far more financially able to consider transitioning out of your business than emotionally ready. Right?"

"I'm not sure exactly how you measure either one, but I'll concede that you are more right than wrong. Financially, I could probably retire today, although not in the lifestyle I'd really want. I have expensive tastes, you know, particularly when I am 'at leisure,'" he laughed. "But my head is clearly not there yet."

"That's understandable," I conceded. "That's why a large part of this process is designed to help you recognize when your 'head *is* there.' As I said, you get to make that call — no one else."

"With your permission, however, let's defer most of our discussion around emotional enthusiasm for now, even though, for many advisors, that's a bigger decision than whether or not they have the financial capacity to transition from their practice.

"In my experience, a big part of any *emotional* uncertainty often stems from anxiety around the *financial* aspects of retirement. So I prefer to deal with the 'money' side first — to give us freedom to address the 'feeling' side. Does that make sense to you?"

"Sure," Henry agreed. "I have the same experience with my clients. Once I get them to accept the realities of their financial situation and what they can realistically expect to accomplish by their targeted retirement date, the focus shifts to the lifestyle they can afford and how to make the most of it — the more emotional side of things, as you describe it."

"And how often, Henry, do they have *un*realistic expectations that you have to bring back to earth," I asked.

"Far too often," Henry lamented. "It continues to amaze me how many people, who have saved virtually nothing throughout their working lives, suddenly think they are going to accumulate enough cash in the five years leading up to their intended retirement date to allow them to continue living the way they have been. In fact, many think they are going to live better — more travel, new hobbies, and so on. It's hard sometimes to be the one who has to break the bad news to them."

"Would it surprise you to learn that many advisors are in the same predicament?" I asked.

"What do you mean?" Henry responded.

"I know this doesn't describe you," I answered, "but regrettably, many advisors have an 'eat-what-you-kill' approach to their business. In other words, they spend all the money they earn and fail to set aside any reasonable amount for their own future needs. In accounting terms, they have no 'retained earnings.'

"These advisors operate what is often referred to as a 'lifestyle practice,' where their entire personal economic security depends on how well their business is doing. If they have a good year, their lifestyle improves; if they have a bad year, their lifestyle suffers because they have no reserves on which to draw to compensate for any decline in their income."

"What's even more distressing," I continued, "is that, because they have little or no personal assets outside their business, many of those same advisors are counting 100% on the sale of their practice to fund their own retirement. And that, unfortunately, isn't likely to work out for them the way they hope it will."

"Why not?" Henry asked. "If it is a 'sellers' market,' as we discussed previously, I am sure someone will buy their book."

"True — there will be buyers. The question, however, becomes, at what price?

"What many of these advisors with lifestyle practices fail to realize is that their businesses aren't worth much without them there because they are built on personal relationships, charisma of the advisor, or some intangible 'halo effect' that is not transferable to a buyer.

"While there is a bit of a feeding frenzy going on right now, potential buyers are becoming increasingly selective about the practices they want. A book of business where much of the goodwill, client relationships, assets, and revenue are at risk of walking out the door at the same time as the advisor will only attract opportunistic buyers looking for a sharply discounted price. Not a great retirement planning strategy, is it?"

"I'm glad you're not talking about me!" Henry reacted. "As we discussed before, I've had several people make overtures about buying my business, and the numbers they are throwing around are, shall I say, 'interesting.'"

"That's a great testament to how well you've built your business over the years. You must have had some good advice and coaching along the way!" I joked.

"If you do say so yourself!" Henry exclaimed.

"More seriously, though," I continued, "do you have a good idea of what your practice is actually worth today? As far as I know, you have never had a proper valuation done. Correct?"

"Nothing formal," Henry admitted, "but don't most practices go for about the same amount — some percentage of assets under management, multiple of revenue, or some such formula?"

"Many practices do trade for so-called 'rules-of-thumb' such as those you describe; however, there is one huge problem with that approach to valuation," I insisted.

"And that is?" Henry asked.

"The assumption that all practices are 'created equal,'" I replied. "I know the answer to this question from the work we have done together in the past, but let me ask you, is there anything about your business that would make it worth more than another one of the same size?"

"I'd like to think so," Henry replied. "I know a few other guys with similar size books, but their business is stressed and chaotic compared to mine. They always seem to be scrambling for clients, trying to find new ways to do things, changing staff, and so on. I don't really have any of those issues. We have good systems in place, a healthy, steady stream of revenue, very loyal clients, and most of our new business comes as a result of referrals from existing clients or centers of influence."

I could not resist the opportunity for another dig at Henry. "More evidence of good advice and coaching!" I exclaimed.

"Humph!" he said, in his now familiar way. "Don't you think *I had something* to do with it too?"

"Of course!" I exclaimed. "You know I'm just kidding. The success you enjoy today is because of you. You're the one who realized that, in today's world, it is no longer sufficient to have a successful advisory practice — you also need to have a sustainable, profitable *business*. Therefore, you were willing to make some tough decisions and implement a strategy to take you to that next level. I provided the process, ideas on industry best practices, and some guidance along the way, as well as the important element of accountability, but you did all the work. You made it happen."

"We are a good team," Henry added.

"Yes, we are," I agreed. "However, before we spend too much time patting each other on the back, let's talk about practice valuation in general. Then we will look more specifically at your business.

"Our firm does a fair number of valuations for practices or books of business being bought or sold every year, so we have seen the good, bad, and the ugly. Here is what I found out very early — both buyers and sellers repeatedly have unrealistic expectations of practice value. Buyers, naturally, always feel they are worth less than sellers do. The bigger problem, however, is that the actual dollar range of values both buyers and sellers are thinking about is often way out of whack. There isn't much realism to their expectations."

"Couldn't that just be negotiation tactics?" Henry asked.

"Some of it is, for sure; however, I have also concluded that, because most advisors have little or no experience buying or selling a practice or book of business, they have no point of reference for price other than those 'rules-of-thumb' you described earlier. In addition, as we said, they rely too much on the *quantitative* measures while ignoring the *qualitative* aspects of a practice.

"Add to that all those 'stories on the street' about transactions that have taken place, and advisors think they have a good idea of practice values. The truth is, however, that buyers are becoming more sophisticated and discerning in what they want. They are engaging professional valuators to dig deep inside a practice to determine its real value. Some practices turn out to be worth much less than the seller wants to believe, and some turn out to be worth much more than the buyer thought they would have to pay."

"And a practice that is extremely well-managed — like mine — would be worth a lot!" Henry speculated with a smile.

"You've got it! Many variables should be considered in valuing an advisory practice. Some are simple *quantitative* measures, while others are more complex, *qualitative* factors. Every practice has nuances that will make it worth more or less than others.

"In fact, when we do a formal valuation, we look at 50–60 different factors, depending on the complexity of the business, which could have an impact on the price someone should be willing to pay. But you have also reminded me to make another important distinction that has a bearing on valuation," I continued.

"And that is?" Henry asked, with increasing interest in his voice.

"We have been talking about buying a book of business and buying a business or practice as if they were the same thing," I answered.

"I've got a feeling you are going to tell me they aren't," Henry offered.

"Even though we often use the terms interchangeably, they *are* different. Buying a *book of business* is simply acquiring a client list and the assets, in-force insurance, etc. that go along with it. Advisors who buy books of business normally just merge those clients into their own client base and systems until the work and identity of the selling advisor disappears completely.

"Buying the *business*, on the other hand, means acquiring the brand and the reputation of the departing advisor. It also often includes retaining the staff and perhaps even the premises, along with systems, technology, and the like. Advisors who buy and integrate active businesses believe they can combine what the founding advisor has built with what they themselves have developed to create synergy — you know — the old 'one-plus-one-equals-three' scenario."

"Obviously," Henry volunteered, "the latter scenario is preferable. After all, as you said, the work we did together previously was designed to do just that — build a sustainable business. I would not be interested in having someone just take over my clients. I'd want them to carry on the business."

"That makes sense for someone like you, Henry," I agreed. "However, there are advisors and situations where it might be more appropriate to simply work out a deal to transfer the clients without transitioning the business."

"I'm having a hard time imagining when that would be," Henry said.

"Well, one scenario would be where a quick sale is required, perhaps because of a death or disability or some other contingency that doesn't really permit the benefit of a longer transition period," I answered.

"The more common situation, however, is the one that I described earlier — the 'lifestyle practice' — where once the original advisor departs, there isn't much left except the client list. The acquiring advisor then takes on the risk of trying to retain those clients and assimilate them into his or her existing business.

"I am not suggesting that one is necessarily a better outcome than the other for any particular advisor, although you can probably guess where my preference would lie. It really is situational. For some retiring advisors who have built lifestyle practices, their best chance at maximizing their payout is to transfer their clients to someone else and pray the purchaser is able to hang onto enough of them to meet the terms of the deal.

"So we are right back to the importance of having a deep-dive analysis done of both the quantitative and qualitative factors of a practice to determine its true value. With that in hand, the founding advisor will have a far better idea of their financial capacity to retire or transition out of the business. It will also make some exit options more practical and appealing than others.

"We'll talk more about the options available to you, Henry, as we go through this process. For now, however, can I start the ball rolling on formally valuing your business?"

"And I assume that the meter starts running at the same time?" Henry joked half-heartedly.

"Yes, of course, there is a fee — it's a lot of work to properly analyze a business like yours," I responded. "The good news, however, is that I already know a lot about your practice, so we'll be able to fast track some parts of the process without compromising it in any way.

"More important, the process will give us up-to-date insight into the opportunities for maximizing the value in your business between now and the date you ultimately decide to hang up your briefcase."

"So you don't think I run a great practice?" Henry shot back.

"What can I say? As your coach, I certainly do!" I replied. "In my experience, however, a periodic review of what makes your business so strong provides an opportunity to fine-tune it even more, making it attractive beyond belief to potential buyers. That will lead to competition among potential suitors and push the price up. But we wouldn't want that, now, would we?"

A small smile cracked Henry's face, and I could tell that he was making mental projections about the value of his business.

Another Illustrative Case in Point

Too Eager to Buy

Doug was so excited I could almost hear his heart pounding through the telephone. We had recently completed a strategic plan to aggressively take his business to a new level. One part of the plan called for him to actively seek out an opportunity to acquire another book of business to complement the organic growth he anticipated from his current practice.

Given that we were in a 'sellers' market,' we knew there would be challenges in finding the right situation and then competing against other potential buyers. We laid out the requirements of what we would consider a 'good book' and put together a plan to let everyone know Doug was interested in making an acquisition and to position him as the preferred candidate.

Now, only a few weeks later, Doug had just received an "out-of-the-blue" call from another advisor in his community who wanted to sell his practice. Furthermore, he said he wanted a quick deal and had selected Doug as his preferred buyer.

The seller had been one of the leading advisors in the community at one time, and although he had slipped from prominence in recent years, he still had a substantial client base. Hence, Doug's urgent call saying that he wanted a quick valuation of the business. The exiting advisor had suggested a price that he said was considerably "below market" because he was anxious to sell in order to move to another part of the country to take care of his aging parents.

When we first contacted the buyer on Doug's behalf to request an interview and financial data, we met with resistance. There was no need, the buyer insisted, for a full valuation. The price offered was well below where other practices of similar size were trading hands. He quoted various "rules-of-thumb" such as percentage of assets and multiple of revenue and even described other practices that had changed hands in the recent past as proof that his price was very attractive and a great opportunity for Doug to leapfrog his business ahead.

Somewhat reluctantly, Doug had agreed that he would only proceed with an offer to purchase if we were able to conduct a reasonably thorough examination of the business and apply standard practice valuation methodology to determine fair value. When informed of this, the founding advisor agreed to meet to describe his business to us and to provide whatever financial information we required.

During the meeting, we discovered:

- Revenue and AUM were up substantially from previous years

- The selling advisor attributed the steady flow of new business to an aggressive marketing campaign

- The firm's "value proposition" described the firm's capabilities as "tax-advantaged investment specialists"

- One tax-advantaged investment product received most of the new sales

- While the firm's AUM was growing at a strong pace, the number of clients was not increasing proportionately

- Financial planning for clients was absent. "Clients want real return... not projections!" was how the seller described his philosophy

Further probing and investigation revealed:

- 40% of client assets were "leveraged" through bank loans and other financing

- In many situations, clients' ability to fund investments was dependent on market performance of one underlying asset

- Tax rules that made the investments "tax-advantaged" were under government review

- The advisor was not looking to sell in order to provide care to his aging parents, but rather due to personal health issues he was experiencing

- The advisor admitted that, as a consequence of his declining health, he had not been servicing his clients as he should have been, and they were increasingly moving their accounts to other advisors

Despite these circumstances, and over our objections, Doug still felt there was something in the business worth salvaging, so we completed our formal valuation and arrived at a value less than half of the seller's already "discounted price." Surprisingly, he accepted the offer and consummated the deal within 60 days.

Doug spent the next 12 months integrating the acquired clients into his business. Fortunately, the markets did not penalize the clients, and the government did not change the tax rules, so a couple of bullets were dodged. Doug did not favor leveraged investing except for the most sophisticated clients who understood and could manage the risks. Consequently, by the end of that year, only about one-third of the original clients remained, either by their choice or by Doug's.

The effort of transitioning clients, adjusting portfolios, and addressing outstanding service issues kept Doug from the activities originally planned to grow his business organically. Essentially, his business ended up in the same place it would have been without acquiring the other book except by a much more difficult path.

The founding advisor did leave the community and has not been heard from since.

Coach's Recap

- Before we can say you are ready to retire or transition out of your practice, two major dimensions of your life situation have to align. The first is your *financial capacity*, and the second is your *emotional enthusiasm*.

- For a transition to be truly successful, you have to score well on both measures. Being financially able but not emotionally enthusiastic is likely to lead to regret about leaving your work behind. On the other hand, being emotionally charged about retirement without the means to enjoy it can be frustrating and demoralizing.

- A large part of any *emotional* uncertainty often stems from anxiety around the *financial* aspects of retirement.

- Many advisors operate a "lifestyle practice," where their entire personal economic security depends on how well their business is doing. If they have a good year, their lifestyle improves; if they have a bad year, their lifestyle suffers because they have no reserves on which to draw to compensate for any decline in their income.

- What many advisors with lifestyle practices fail to realize is that their businesses are not worth much without them there because they are built on personal relationships, charisma of the advisor, or some other intangible that is not transferable to a buyer.

- Regrettably, because they have little or no personal assets outside their business, many advisors with lifestyle practices are counting entirely on the sale of their practice to fund their own retirement. Unfortunately, that isn't likely to work out for them the way they hope it will.

- Potential buyers are becoming increasingly selective about the practices they want. A book of business where much of the goodwill, client relationships, assets, and revenue are at risk of walking out the door at the same time as the advisor will only attract opportunistic buyers looking for a sharply discounted price.

- Both buyers and sellers have unrealistic expectations of practice value. Buyers, naturally, usually feel they are worth less than sellers do. Secondly, the range of values both buyers and sellers are thinking about is often misguided.

- Because most advisors have little or no experience buying or selling a practice or book of business, they have no point of reference for price other than "rules-of-thumb," which assume all practices are "created equal." (They are not!)

- Buying *a book of business* is simply acquiring a client list and the assets, in-force insurance, etc. that go along with it. Advisors who buy books of business normally just merge those clients into their own client base and systems until the work and identity of the selling advisor disappears completely.

- Buying a *business*, on the other hand, means acquiring the brand and the reputation of the departing advisor. It also often includes retaining the staff and perhaps even the premises, along with systems, technology, and the like. Advisors who buy and integrate active businesses believe they can combine what the founding advisor has built with what they themselves have developed to create synergy.

My Succession Plan

Exercise #2 – Practice Valuation

1. **When the time is right, I will sell:**
   - ☐ My 'book of business'
   - ☐ My 'business'

2. **My reason for choosing my answer in Question #1 above is**

   _____

   _____

3. **I think my practice is best described as:** (Choose most accurate description)
   - ☐ A good job that pays me a fair wage for the work I do
   - ☐ A "lifestyle practice" that pays me an above-average compensation
   - ☐ A "sustainable business" that is creating long-term value
   - ☐ A significant enterprise with substantial value today
   - ☐ Other (Specify)_____

4. **My practice has been valued by:**
   - ☐ Me, according to a "rule-of-thumb" e.g. multiple of revenue, % of AUM
   - ☐ Me, according to "what I have heard on the street'
   - ☐ My dealer firm's formula
   - ☐ A professional valuator
   - ☐ Someone who is/was interested in buying it
   - ☐ Other (Specify) _____

5. **The value of my practice today is:**
   - ☐ More than enough to fund my retirement
   - ☐ Enough to fund my retirement
   - ☐ Not enough to fund my retirement
   - ☐ I don't know what the real value of my practice is today

6. **My experience in buying or selling a practice of book of business is:**
   - ☐ Considerable
   - ☐ Modest
   - ☐ Limited
   - ☐ None

"Price is what you pay… Value is what you get."
Warren Buffett

Chapter 3

What is my practice worth?

"So what types of things are you looking for when you do a practice valuation?" Henry asked.

"Good question," I answered. "As I said before, we look at a business from two perspectives — quantitative and qualitative. The quantitative part is straightforward; that's just crunching the numbers around things like revenue, cash flow, and so on.

"The qualitative aspects are much more subjective and vary with each practice. And quite frankly, they are often more important than the numbers themselves because they represent the unique characteristics of a business that could make it worth more or less than others."

"Can you give me an example?"

"Sure, let me speak to both sides of the ledger — quantitative and qualitative — because they both lie at the heart of practice valuation. Let's start with the numbers side.

"Here's the #1 underlying fundamental principle of practice valuation — **the current value of a financial advisory practice is determined by its expected future profitability — not past results**. Why do I put such an emphasis on this? Because it presents a problem for advisors who are looking to sell their practices by touting their past records as proof of the value of their business. They are looking through the wrong end of the telescope.

"Obviously, as a buyer, I am interested in how a practice has performed previously because it tells me about its momentum and how well it has been managed. However, what the business earned in the past was the original advisor's return on their investment in the business — both their 'sweat equity' and any financial contribution they made.

"Similarly, the price I am willing to pay for the business today should be based on the expected return on *my* investment, that is, the profits I think the practice can generate after I have acquired it.

"Besides, what do you always tell your clients about past performance?"

"That it is no guarantee of future results," Henry responded robotically.

"Good for you!" I congratulated him mischievously. "That's another reason I don't like 'rules-of-thumb' — they all look backwards instead of forward."

I continued, "The second important principle of valuation is that **cash flow is king**! Aside from a bit of furniture and a few pieces of office equipment, the only real asset most advisors have in their business is their client base. Unfortunately, from an accounting perspective, the value of their client base does not appear on their Balance Sheet except in some indirect way as goodwill.

"Where the value of that client base does show up, however, is on the Income or Profit and Loss Statement in the form of the cash flow that is generated by that client base. Hence, cash flow represents the major asset an advisor has to offer for sale. Everything else — equipment, systems, brand, reputation, expertise, etc. are simply support items for generating cash flow.

"So, bearing in mind Principle #1 — that future profitability is the only thing that determines value — and Principle #2 — that cash flow is what counts, the best basis on which to value a practice is to measure the expected cash flow that is left after all the expenses required to run the business have been paid. Am I making sense so far?"

"Sure — the value of the business is the present value of its future profits, like any other investment," Henry concluded.

"I wish I'd said it that simply," I responded.

"But here's my question," Henry continued. "What constitutes profitability in an advisory practice? After paying my operating expenses, staff, and so on and leaving a bit in the business for short-term cash needs and emergencies, I take the rest home as my personal compensation — essentially there are no 'profits' left, so to speak. Is what I earn considered my 'profit'?"

"An excellent question! And the answer is 'Yes, partially' — because you actually get paid in two ways. Part of what you take home is your profit as the owner of your business. The other part is your compensation for being an advisor."

"I'm not sure I'm following this."

"Let me try to better explain.

"Your compensation as an advisor is actually an expense to the business, based on the simple assumption that your business couldn't operate without someone performing the advisor's role. In your case, you are that person. In other practices where there are a number of advisors working, their costs, including compensation, would be charged as direct expenses to the business before any profit was calculated.

"So you should be paid fair compensation for your advisor work, and that expense should be deducted from revenue like any other expense to determine profitability. Once that is done, as owner of the business, you should then be rewarded for the risks you have taken and the effort you have invested in building the business. You receive that reward out of profits."

"I have never really thought about it that way," Henry admitted, "but it makes sense to me. Advisor compensation is a legitimate expense to the business. Anything else I take home is my owner compensation."

"Most advisors don't make the distinction," I added, "but it is essential for valuation purposes. Otherwise, the business's true profitability can't be calculated.

"Think about your early years in the business. You didn't earn any 'profits,' so to speak, so you didn't receive any 'owner compensation.' Your personal income came from your job as an advisor. Over time, however, more and more of your revenue started to come from ongoing fees, renewals, referrals, larger accounts — all results of building a great business. You started to pay yourself more each year — not because you necessarily deserved more as an advisor, but because you deserved to earn owner compensation.

"And as the proprietor of a profitable business, you get to choose how the excess cash flow above expenses will be used. You can reinvest it in the business — or pay it to yourself so you can buy a new boat, or do whatever you choose.

"Because you have discretion over the use of the profits, we refer to that cash flow as 'discretionary cash flow,' and it is the basis on which most financial advisory practices are valued. More technically, the calculation is the present value of future discretionary cash flow. Did I do a better job of describing that one?"

"Sure," Henry said mockingly. "My practice is worth the present value of a future stream of earnings, the same way we price bonds and annuities, etc."

"Augh!" I said. "Will you give me lessons in stating things simply?"

"Well, it does seem pretty straightforward," Henry laughed. "But I do have one question. If most advisors, including me, don't think about separating their personal income into advisor compensation and owner compensation, how does someone valuing a practice decide on the appropriate split? Obviously, a 60/40 split would result in a significantly different valuation than a 40/60 split."

"Another good question! When we value a practice, regardless of how much the advisor pays himself or herself in total, we'll allocate a reasonable cost to having someone perform the work of an advisor as if we had to hire them."

"So how do you determine a reasonable cost for 'advisor compensation'?"

"That varies with the size and complexity of the business," I answered. "We look at the number of clients the advisor is serving and the type of work being done. If the advisor is doing comprehensive planning and actively managing large portfolios for a significant number of clients, we'll assume there is a higher cost associated with delivering that level of service than there would be for an advisor who does only basic planning and has all of their clients invested in mutual funds."

"Well, the first advisor is doing a better job, so they should be paid more," Henry jumped in.

"I'm not even suggesting that," I countered. "All I'm saying is that there are probably higher level skills required and more costs involved in the first example. Fortunately, there are industry averages that we can also use as benchmarks. You might be interested to know that the typical range for 'advisor compensation' is $100,000 to $350,000 per year, depending on the situation."

I could tell the wheels were turning in Henry's head as he mentally calculated his income compared to those numbers.

"But this highlights a problem for those advisors with lifestyle practices such as we talked about before. Chances are, they are being rewarded mostly for their advisor role and marginally, if at all, for their ownership.

"That explains why a lifestyle practice may not attract a great price when the founder decides to exit the business. It is a common misconception among advisors that their practice is worth some big multiple of their personal income. A smart purchaser, however, will argue for a low price based on the fact they have to pay someone else to do the advisor's work, leaving little or no discretionary cash flow."

"And no discretionary cash flow means no value," Henry concluded.

"Theoretically, that would be accurate. The truth of the matter, however, as we discussed, is that in today's market, there is always someone around willing to buy just about any book of business. The price may not be what the advisor was hoping for, so they they'll probably have to make some lifestyle changes when they leave the business."

"And I am not sure many are prepared for that," Henry suggested.

"Unfortunately, I believe you are right.

"Now, I suggest a short break, after which I'd like to explore the 'qualitative' side of the valuation equation so I can further answer your question about the things we look for when doing a valuation. This side is considerably more complex than the numbers side, and as I said earlier, it can have a much greater impact on final price.

When we reconvened, I summarized our earlier conversation.

"So, now we know that the value of an advisory practice is the present value of future profits or what is referred to as discretionary cash flow.

"If that were all we had to worry about, our work as valuators would be simple. However, unlike the bonds or annuities you used as examples earlier, which have stated interest rates on which to base the calculation of present value, future cash flow and profitability of a financial advisory practice is uncertain for all the reasons we both know.

"That uncertainty brings the whole question of risk/reward trade-off into the picture. So, in answer to your question of what we look for in a valuation, we look for the qualitative characteristics of the practice that would either increase or decrease the risk that the discretionary cash flow will not materialize as expected. Then we adjust our valuation accordingly.

"As the potential, someday seller of your business, you should be aware of the various risk factors and how to mitigate them. Anything you can do to reduce risk to a purchaser should warrant a higher price.

"Such as?" Henry asked.

"Increasing net cash flow will work every time," I said. "More discretionary cash flow leads to higher valuations.

"Even though we stated this before, it is such an important factor that it is worth repeating — increasing recurring revenue reduces uncertainty around cash flow, thereby reducing risk and improving valuation.

"Having an up-to-date strategic plan that a prospective buyer can take and run with to continue to grow the business adds value.

"Having a plan to attract younger clients to replace those whose needs have all been met or who die assures ongoing vitality for the business.

"Having a defined brand in your marketplace that is recognized by your target market gives a buyer instant recognition and leverage.

"Reducing operating expenses through efficiency or scale helps with profitability, as does lowering client acquisition and service costs.

"Improving productivity, for example, average revenue per account, per client, per team member, and so on, demonstrates effectiveness.

"Following a client segmentation process that matches client value to service levels contributes to productivity and profitability.

"Having up-to-date client records reduces compliance risk and improves productivity."

"You know it never really occurred to me before," Henry interjected, "but wasn't the work we did in the past largely to improve the qualitative aspects of my business like those you have just described."

"You are right," I agreed. "It may not have directly appeared so at the time, but everything we did when we last worked together was designed to maximize the value of your business. Do you remember what I called my 'management mantra'?"

"How could I forget — you made me repeat it so many times," Henry teased. "Run your business as if it will last forever, but be prepared to sell it *at any time* to the *most qualified buyer* for the *highest price.*"

"Excellent — you even had the emphasis in the right places," I congratulated him.

"But seriously, 'life happens,' and we just never know when circumstances or desire might cause us to leave the business. It must give you confidence knowing that your practice is highly efficient and very profitable and that the things you did to make it so will serve you well when you decide to transition out."

"It does, indeed," Henry admitted. "At the time, I wasn't thinking about retirement, but I can now see how that scenario, even if it is ten years away, will be much better as a result of what we did five or six years ago."

"What's also very interesting to me after all these years of coaching is how getting the qualitative aspects of your business in good order almost automatically translates into an increase in the quantitative parts.

"Which brings me to the final point I want to make today — the importance of having accurate financial information that reflects the true value of the business.

"Obviously, when we do valuations, we need to review the business's financial statements. That is why I am surprised to find so many financial advisors without proper accounting records. In many instances, the closest they come to having financial statements at all are those prepared by their accountants for income tax purposes. Think about it — what is the objective with statements for income tax calculation purposes — it is to reduce the advisor's income to its lowest level to attract the least amount of tax.

"That's exactly opposite to what you want to illustrate when selling your business. Then you want to show the greatest amount of income you can to receive the highest valuation. Part of our job when we do valuations is to 'normalize' the financials by backing out all the 'creative accounting' such as family members on the payroll, vacations posing as business trips, personal expenditures disguised as business expenses, and so on."

"No problem," Henry said. "My accountant is a great guy, but he is a real straight arrow and stickler for accuracy. I have no concerns there."

"Excellent!" I said.

"We've covered a lot of ground today, Henry, and I think, come a long way in our discussion," I said.

"Let's both take some time to reflect on your state of financial readiness as far as your retirement strategy goes. I will do my bit by getting started on a formal valuation of your business. You give some thought to your situation outside the business. With that information in hand, we'll be better prepared to discuss the emotional aspects of retirement in our next session. Does that make sense to you?"

"It does," Henry answered simply. I could tell by the faraway look in his eyes, however, that he was thinking, calculating, and visualizing.

Another Illustrative Case in Point

Diminishing Value

Clancy was an old-school financial advisor who had been in the business for forty years. He started as a life insurance agent collecting premiums on a "debit" and picking up small policy sales along the way. Eventually, he moved to a career branch of his firm, where he stayed for almost 20 years.

Clancy was very close to his Branch Manager, so when that manager retired, Clancy decided to leave the branch office and work from his home. He obtained his mutual fund license, joined an independent dealer firm with a higher payout schedule, and over the next 15 years, built a simple, but comfortable practice advising clients on their insurance policies and investments. Clancy loved working from home and saw most of his clients at their homes or places of business. His wife did his bookkeeping and filing while Clancy focused on preparing and presenting investment proposals and insurance illustrations for prospective and current clients.

When he started to feel the effects of age, Clancy began to seriously consider retirement. He was not sure what he would do when he retired, but he sensed it was time to move on. The industry was changing at a pace he found a bit dizzying. Compliance was becoming an increasing burden, the firm's technology intimidated him, new regulations were confusing, and clients seemed to be becoming less "friendly."

He had not really thought too much about selling his business. His former company did not permit him to sell because they deemed him to be an "employee" whose clients belonged to the firm. At a recent conference of his current firm, however, he heard lots of talk about advisors wanting to buy books of business. The "going rate" seemed to be two to three times revenue, which, given Clancy's average income in recent years of $200,000, should yield him a selling price somewhere in the half-a-million-dollar range. While it would not make him rich, that would be enough for Clancy to maintain his relatively simple lifestyle in retirement.

The firm had a contract with a professional financial advisory practice valuator to do valuations at a reduced fee, so Clancy engaged him to determine a fair price for his business. Even though he knew he could easily sell his book of business, Clancy, of course, wanted to get the highest price possible, so he hoped the valuator would be able to demonstrate that Clancy's long-standing client base, assets under management, and in-force insurance would warrant a premium price.

Unfortunately for Clancy, the exact opposite occurred. The valuator found that:

- Revenue had been declining at about 5% per year, and the rate of decline was accelerating as clients outgrew their need for more products, passed their assets to children with whom Clancy had no relationship, died, or left to join other advisors

- Average age of the clients was 67

- Only one-third of revenue was recurring service fees and insurance renewals; the balance was commissions on new sales

- Almost all new sales came from existing relationships; very few new clients had been added in recent years

- Client records were incomplete and disorganized; some contained out-of-date information

- Client service was "on-demand" and reactive

While the "quantitative" side of Clancy's business looked good from the outside, a deeper evaluation revealed weaknesses on the "qualitative" aspects.

The result was a valuation of $225,000, just slightly more than one times Clancy's annual income. Furthermore, the value of the business was likely to continue to decline, leaving him with the choice of selling now and accepting the reality of a dramatically reduced lifestyle or waiting for the inevitable total evaporation of his largest financial asset.

Coach's Recap

- Financial advisory practices are evaluated from two perspectives — quantitative and qualitative. The quantitative part is straightforward: things like revenue, cash flow, and so on.

- The qualitative aspects are much more subjective and vary with each practice. They are often more important than the numbers themselves because they represent the unique characteristics of a business that could make it worth more or less than others.

- The #1 underlying fundamental principle of practice valuation is that the **expected future profitability — not past results — determines the current value of a financial advisory practice**

- The price someone is willing to pay for a practice should be based on the expected return on their investment, that is, the profits they think the practice can generate after they acquire it.

- The second important principle of valuation is that **cash flow is king**! The only real asset most advisors have in their business is their client base. Unfortunately, the value of their client base does not appear on their Balance Sheet.

- The value of that client base does show up on the Income or Profit and Loss Statement in the form of the cash flow generated by that client base. Hence, cash flow represents the major asset an advisor has to offer for sale.

- The best basis on which to value a practice is to measure the expected cash flow that is left after all the expenses, including advisor compensation, required to run the business have been paid.

- Independent financial advisors are paid in two ways: first, for their work as advisors (advisor compensation) and, second, for their profit as the owners of their businesses (owner compensation).

- Because you have discretion over the use of the profit, it is referred to as "discretionary cash flow" and is the basis on which most financial advisory practices are valued.

- The actual calculation is the present value of future discretionary cash flow.

- It is a common misconception among advisors that their practice is worth some big multiple of their personal income. Chances are, advisors with lifestyle practices are being compensated for their advisor role and marginally, if it all, for their ownership.

- A smart purchaser will argue for a low price based on the fact they have to pay someone else to do the advisor's work, leaving little or no discretionary cash flow.

- Unlike bonds or annuities, which have stated interest rates on which to base the calculation of present value, future cash flow and profitability of a financial advisory practice is uncertain.

- That uncertainty brings the trade-off between risk and reward into the picture. Professional valuators look for the qualitative characteristics of a practice that would either increase or decrease the risk that the discretionary cash flow will not materialize as expected and adjust their valuation accordingly.

- You can reduce risk (and therefore increase value) by:
  - Having an up-to-date strategic plan
  - Increasing net cash flow
  - Increasing percentage of recurring revenue
  - Having a plan to attract younger clients
  - Having a defined brand in your marketplace
  - Reducing operating expenses, client acquisition, and service costs
  - Improving average revenue per account, per client, per team member
  - Implementing a client segmentation process that matches client value to service levels
  - Having up-to-date client records
  - Having accurate financial information

- Decisions you make around preparing for succession will serve your business well anytime.

- Run your business as if it will last forever, but always be prepared to sell it *at any time* to the *most qualified buyer for the highest price.*

My Succession Plan

Exercise #3 – Improving Value

1. On a scale of 1-10, (1 = Poor; 10 = Excellent), I would rate my practice today on its *"quantitative"* appeal to a potential buyer as

    _____

2. The "quantitative" things I could improve to increase the value of my practice are: (Check all that apply)
    - ☐ Increase overall cash flow
    - ☐ Reduce operating costs
    - ☐ Increase the percentage of recurring revenue
    - ☐ Increase pricing
    - ☐ Improve "turn rate" i.e. return on assets (ROA)
    - ☐ Improve productivity e.g. average account size, # clients per staff, etc.
    - ☐ Improve client retention rate
    - ☐ Other (Specify) _____
    - ☐ Other (Specify) _____

3. On a scale of 1-10, (1 = Poor; 10 = Excellent), I would rate my practice today on its "qualitative" appeal to a potential buyer as

    _____

4. The *"qualitative"* things I could improve to increase the value of my practice are: (Check all that apply)
    - ☐ Have an up-to-date strategic plan
    - ☐ Diversify my revenue sources
    - ☐ Develop a program to attract younger clients
    - ☐ Define and communicate my brand
    - ☐ Implement a better client segmentation strategy
    - ☐ Have more complete client records
    - ☐ Have accurate and up-to-date financial records
    - ☐ Other (Specify) _____
    - ☐ Other (Specify) _____

5. My total compensation this year will be $ _____
    a. Of that total, I think a fair amount for my "advisor comp" is $ _____
    b. Of that total, I think a fair amount for my "owner comp" is $ _____

"When one door closes, another opens; but we often look so long and so regretfully upon the closed door that we do not see the one which has opened for us."
Alexander Graham Bell

Chapter 4

How do I prepare myself?

Fortunately, as Henry mentioned, he and his accountant had kept good financial records for his business. Consequently, it did not take nearly as long as it typically would for many advisors to gather the quantitative information needed to do a proper valuation of his business. He was readily able to supply us with all the data we needed with respect to assets under management, revenue, expenses, product mix, compensation, and other measureable inputs to our calculations.

I also knew quite a bit about Henry's practice because of our past work; however, we still insisted on conducting our detailed analysis of the qualitative factors that might make his business worth more or less than another.

It took almost three weeks to complete our valuation and report, which we had already delivered to Henry. He seemed quite pleased with our estimate of the value of his business today, so it was perfect timing to move our earlier discussions along from his financial capacity to transition out of his business to his emotional enthusiasm to move on to the next chapter in his life.

"You must be both happy and proud of what you've accomplished so far with your business, Henry," I began after we had settled in his boardroom for our next formal session. "You have built a successful, profitable, and efficient business that is well-positioned to provide you with financial security for as long as you choose to be part of it. And when that day comes that you decide it is time to transition to the next phase of your life, you can count on your business to support a nice lifestyle."

"It is a good feeling to see what my business is worth in writing," Henry admitted with a smile, "and to know that the value will only grow! It gives me much better perspective on my future options that I hadn't really thought about before."

"And it changes your mood as well, I can see," I joked.

"But let's not get too carried away. A lot can happen to your business between now and then — some good things, some not so good. The real test will be what your business is worth on the day you decide to sell it. In fact, it goes even further than that — it is what someone will be willing to pay you for it at that time. Regardless of what value I put on a piece of paper for your practice, the final price will be determined by how anxious you are to sell and how motivated a buyer is to acquire your business over all the others that will be available at that time."

"Yeah, but my practice will be more attractive than many. You said so yourself," Henry countered. "So I don't have to be 'anxious to sell' at all — I can just wait for the right buyer to come along."

"I'll give you that your business *should* be at the top of many buyers' lists," I replied.

"Humph," was Henry's now familiar response to things he'd rather not discuss further, so I decided to give him something more specific and, hopefully, more fun to think about.

"Now that you have an idea of what your practice is worth today and, I am guessing, some thoughts about what it could be worth in the future, how far along do you feel you are from being in a financial position to retire to that expensive lifestyle you said you had when you were 'at leisure'?" I asked.

"Funny thing about that," Henry bounced back quickly. "Now that I do have that sense of the value of my business, I have found myself thinking a little differently about what I'd like my transition from the business to look like."

"How so?" I asked.

"Well, initially, it was all about me — the lifestyle I wanted, the travel, the good things in life — you know what I mean," he trailed off.

"Ah, the hedonistic retiree," I teased him.

"Yeah, something like that," Henry shot back, clearly not pleased I had labeled him as self-indulgent in any way.

He continued, "I agree with the old cliché that 'money can't buy happiness,' but what it can provide is choice. If the value of my practice eventually gets to be something like I think is possible in a few years, there are lots of things I could do instead of just taking the money so I can golf every day or lie on a beach somewhere."

"What sort of things do you have in mind?" I asked.

"I'm not totally sure yet," he said, "but I'd like to 'give back' in some way — to the industry, to the community, to someone or something that could use a helping hand."

"I have no doubt, Henry, that you'd have all kinds of opportunities to make the world a better place in some way," I offered. "With your intellect, work ethic, and management skills, people would line up to take advantage of anything you wanted to give."

"Now don't get me wrong," Henry jumped in. "I still want to enjoy life and the nice things that money can buy, but if I were in a financial position to help others as well, that would be great."

Henry's newfound enthusiasm and energy were both welcome, and I certainly did not want to dampen either; however, as his coach, I felt compelled to bring some specificity and perspective to his ambitions.

"So what I hear you saying is that you may not be as financially prepared for retirement as you thought. It's not that you have suddenly gotten poor or greedy — in fact, quite the opposite, obviously — you feel your business is worth more, and as a result, you have become more generous. So you've 'raised the bar,' so to speak, on what it would take to allow you to fully enjoy your retirement."

"That's not a bad thing," Henry said half questioningly.

"Not at all!" I responded. "How could wanting to work towards the benefit of others ever be a bad thing?

"Let me provide a little perspective from my experience in trying to get other advisors to determine how financially prepared they are to retire.

"Think of a continuum of financial capability that ranges from low to medium to high. On the low end, we have those advisors with the extreme lifestyle practices that we described earlier, where their personal economic viability depends entirely on how well their business is doing. In good years, they prosper; in bad years, they suffer. Because they have little or no investments outside of their business, they are counting on the sale of their practice or book of business to fund their retirement.

"In most instances, these advisors are not financially prepared to retire. At best, they might be able to sell their business for, say, two to three times the income they had been earning — that is funding for only two to three years of retirement unless they sharply reduce their personal spending.

"Not surprisingly, these advisors are also often the ones least prepared *emotionally* to exit the business because they know their own retirement picture isn't all that rosy."

"I know guys like that," Henry interjected. "They say they will never retire because they enjoy what they do too much, but I bet the truth for many is that they can't afford to retire."

"And that's a sad thing for someone who counsels others on retirement planning to admit," I added.

"But let's move to the other end of the spectrum — those advisors who are well-prepared financially to retire. They typically have substantial personal assets outside their business, so they do not need to sell their practices to maintain their lifestyle in retirement. In fact, for many of those advisors, what happens to their clients is more important than the money.

"As you might guess, advisors at this end of the continuum are often also the most prepared *emotionally* to transition out of their business. As you indicated, wealth gives them the freedom to do other things that are meaningful in their lives."

"I don't think I'm quite in that position — yet!" Henry said with emphasis.

"Fortunately, my financial obligations are not onerous and, between what I now know is my 'advisor compensation' and my 'owner compensation,' my practice pays me more than enough to support my lifestyle. So I have been able to build some personal assets to supplement proceeds from the sale of my business; however, I am still counting on selling my practice to fund a significant part of my retirement."

"That's great," I congratulated him. "You are somewhere in the middle of the range — and quite frankly; I think that is the best place to be. It means you are not desperate and you have a solid foundation on which to continue to build your business. Because there is still work to be done to maximize the value in your practice between now and the date you ultimately decide to transition out, you can still shape your legacy to be the one you want.

"You've given us a bit of a picture of what you want your retirement to look like — with you 'giving back.' Now you get to decide when you will be financially ready to do that. In the interim, we'll keep working to add to the value of your business."

Henry sat quietly for a moment, and my guess was that his vision for retirement was beginning to crystalize. Finally, he spoke. "Yes, I like that approach," was all he said as he excused himself for a washroom break, but I was pretty sure there was more going through Henry's mind than his physical comfort.

When Henry returned to the boardroom, I decided it was appropriate for us to take our conversation in a related, but slightly different direction. So I began by saying, "You've no doubt noticed, Henry, that I have repeatedly paired being ready to retire *financially* with being prepared *emotionally*, so I think we should talk a bit about that aspect of succession as well."

"Yes," he acknowledged, "and I recall you saying in one of our earlier sessions that for a transition to be truly successful, you have to score well on both measures. And I can see more clearly now, as you also said, that being financially sound would help on the emotional side of things."

"Excellent — so let's dig a little deeper into this," I suggested, "because, in my experience, it is often the psychological side of the equation that prevents advisors from being more proactive with their exit strategy."

"I think you might be talking about me now," Henry said, only partially in jest.

"You and three out of four other advisors," I responded. "And I get it — for many entrepreneurs, their business is what inspires them and gives them that get-up-and-go feeling every morning. They have a hard time imagining their lives without that 'fire in the belly' driving them.

"Financial advisors can be afflicted even more because of the nature of their work. In some ways, what you do is more like a 'calling' than a job. You get deeply involved with people's personal lives and care a lot about their well-being. Your role as a confidant, counsellor, and cheerleader gives you vigor and enthusiasm.

"So to help with the issue of whether or not they are ready emotionally to exit their business, I suggest advisors ask themselves a number of questions, such as, 'How much of my energy comes from my role as an advisor? Would I be OK with someone else taking care of my clients? Will I miss the "action"? Will I miss the people? Will I miss the public profile? Do I have something else to "retire to"?'"

"I do admit, I'd have trouble with some of those questions," Henry offered. "This is a 24/7 job — watching the economy and the markets, reacting to client needs, staying up-to-date professionally, always being on the lookout for new business opportunities — I love it partly because of that 'action.' It *does* give me energy, but at the same time, it consumes a lot of energy. How do you measure something like that to decide 'now is the time'?"

"Because this is so subjective and personal, it's not like crunching the numbers to determine if you are financially prepared," I conceded. "So think again, just as we did for financial capacity, about there being a range or continuum of emotional enthusiasm that extends from low to medium to high.

"On the low end of the scale are those advisors who are totally defined by their business. You know the type — they eat, sleep, and breathe the markets and anything related to what they do for clients. They can hardly carry on a conversation about much else."

"I find those people somewhat annoying," Henry said. "I love my work and my clients, but there is more to life than my practice. *I* don't even like spending too much time with advisors who simply go on and on about their business as if nothing else was important. I can imagine how people around them must feel."

"I happen to agree with you," I said, "but I am not sure those advisors can help it.

"Their business is their life, and their life is their business, so they have no idea what else they'd do with their time. They enjoy the 'perks' that come with the job — being their own boss, flexible hours, business paying for some personal expenses and so on. They are also often driven by the recognition they feel they receive for their knowledge and work to the point where they feel they could not survive without the business and vice versa. Unfortunately, they are often right about the business not surviving without them, which is not a good thing if they are contemplating a sale."

"Those advisors shouldn't ever be thinking about selling — they'd die!" Henry exclaimed.

"Well, I'm not sure they'd expire physically," I responded, "but they'd certainly suffer psychologically.

"But let's move to the other end of the spectrum — to those advisors who are ready to make the transition. Typically, they are very proud of what they have accomplished in their business, but they frequently have some other passion in life they would like to pursue. Perhaps it is a hobby, more time with the family, travel, or whatever. They often want to share their knowledge or 'give back' to the industry by coaching or mentoring someone to carry on in their place. Sound like anyone you know, Henry?"

"Well, that certainly sounds a lot more like me than the other group of advisors you described! But I'm not sure I'm there — yet," Henry reacted emphatically, as he had previously. "I still enjoy my work very much, and besides, I haven't defined exactly what it is I want to do when I retire. I just know I'd feel good about helping someone somehow."

"Then I'd suggest that you are once again in the middle of the scale," I offered. "That's where we put advisors who feel their life extends beyond their practice and who'd like more time to pursue other interests. They are content with what they have accomplished and still find fun in the business. They often have a good support team in place, so they are starting to enjoy more freedom around how they spend their time. Are we getting closer to describing you, Henry?"

"Yes, that's better — well beyond the first group, but not quite at the high end of the scale," Henry agreed.

"Again, I think that is a great place for you to be right now," I said, "given that we agreed you also weren't fully prepared financially for your newly elevated exit plan. I have a very strong feeling that by the time you are ready on the money side, you will also be motivated emotionally because you will have a much better definition of what you want to do to 'give back.' Does that make sense to you?"

"I'm beginning to get the picture," Henry volunteered.

"Speaking of pictures, you know I've never met a whiteboard or flipchart I didn't like, so do you mind if I draw us a little diagram to illustrate what we have just been talking about?" I asked.

"Go ahead, Professor," Henry laughed.

"Thanks," I said. "Let's first draw a horizontal line to represent what we'll call 'Financial Freedom' — the *ability* to *afford* to retire in the way you want, with Low on the left, Medium in the middle, and High on the right, like this.

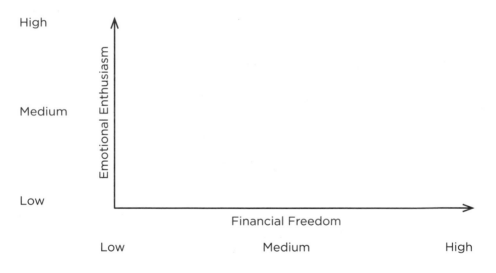

"Now let's draw a vertical line to represent 'Emotional Enthusiasm' — the *willingness* to retire, with Low on the bottom, Medium in the middle, and High at the top, like this.

"Now let's divide diagram this into four quadrants to create what I call the Financial/Emotional Matrix. Does that sound professorial, or what?" I joked.

Financial/Emotional Matrix[1]

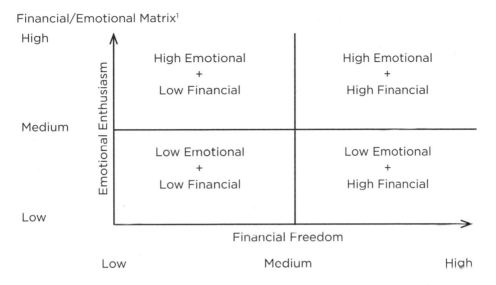

"In the bottom left corner, we have those advisors who are, as the popular saying goes, *'stuck between a rock and a hard place.'* They have little financial freedom or emotional enthusiasm to retire. Perhaps the two are related. Regardless, advisors who fall into this quadrant have a lot of work to do to get ready for their eventual exit from the business. If I had colored pens, I would shade this corner of the matrix red for 'Danger.'

"In the top left corner are advisors who are anxious to leave the business but can't really afford to. The good news for them is that, with some effort and a sensible plan, they can increase the value of their business to improve their financial freedom to choose when they exit. The challenge for many advisors in this position, however, is being patient through the changes they have to make. For that reason, if I had colored pens, I would shade this section yellow for 'Caution.'

"The bottom-right quadrant is where we find advisors who can afford to exit but they just don't want to. They may be really enjoying their work, don't know what they'd do next, or, in some cases, are grooming a successor, often a family member who they don't feel is ready to take over the business completely. These advisors have the advantage of being able to wait until they are emotionally ready to exit because the financial aspect is not as much of an issue for them. That said, I would color this corner yellow for 'Caution' as well. I have seen a number of advisors jump at a big offer for their business that left them financially well off but mentally unprepared to leave their life's work behind. The result was regret and unhappiness.

---

1   Derived from John Leonetti's book *Exiting Your Business, Protecting Your Wealth* www.pinnacleequitysolutions.com

"Finally, in the top right corner, we have those advisors who score high on both dimensions. They are equipped both psychologically and financially to do whatever they choose. While they may be ready to go, they don't have to, and yet, when they decide the time is right, they can just pull the trigger on their retirement. These advisors have the luxury of choice, so I would make this quadrant green for 'Go.'

"So, Henry, where would you place yourself on this grid?" I asked.

Henry stared at my rough drawing for a full minute or so before answering.

"Well, as we agreed earlier, I seem to fit in the middle of both lines, so I guess that puts me in the center of your diagram," he finally said.

"Yeah, I'd agree to some extent," I said. "However, I think you are a little to the right and above the center point — definitely in the 'green zone' but not as deep as you'd like to be before making your exit. Does that seem right to you?"

"It does," Henry replied. "In the 'go-forward' zone — but not the 'go' zone — yet!"

The emphasis with which Henry made that statement let me know that he was starting to accept the challenge of getting himself better prepared to transition from his business. I suggested a coffee break to allow that feeling to grow.

Another Illustrative Case in Point

Retire "to" Something

Mary was well known in the industry as a leader and achiever. She had started as an advisor at a time when few women made that a career choice. She eventually became a Branch Manager and then spent several years in executive positions in her company's Head Office. Her passion, however, was working with clients, so she decided to spend the last ten years or so of her career as an advisor.

She purchased a small practice from a retiring advisor, which she ultimately built into a great business specializing in working with female entrepreneurs. In addition, Mary became heavily involved in the industry's advisor association, ultimately rising to become National President and then Chair of the Board of Directors.

Mary had always told everyone around her that she would be retiring at age 65, while she was still young enough to travel, enjoy her hobbies, and spoil her grandchildren. Two years before that milestone birthday, Mary entered into an agreement with two of the other advisors in her office (whom she had recruited and mentored) to acquire the business. Proceeds from the sale, combined with her personal assets, meant Mary would not have to worry about meeting her lifestyle ambitions.

When the big day finally arrived, there was huge celebration at Mary's office. Clients came to congratulate her, company executives thanked her for her loyalty, industry leaders praised her contributions, and staff and associates wished her well in retirement. It seemed like a fitting end to a great career.

Six months later, after returning from a three-week cruise, Mary woke up one morning with a deep sense of regret. She missed the business — a lot. She wished she could still have the kind of deep and intimate conversations she used to with clients about their life goals and how to achieve them. She longed for the satisfaction of coaching team members towards their career objectives. She wanted the kind of intellectual stimulation she used to get from working at high levels on important issues that were going to shape the future of the industry. In short, Mary missed "the buzz" that surrounded her career for so many years.

What became clear to Mary was that she should not have retired so abruptly from the business she loved so much. Circling her 65th birthday on the calendar as the day she would cease all involvement was a mistake. It failed to take into account the fact that she might not be emotionally prepared to leave behind her life's work at that time. It also assumed she would have something to do after retiring that would provide her with the same personal enjoyment and psychic reward.

Mary knew that she could not "go back" to the way things had been. Her business had been sold, and she was subject to a non-competition clause in the agreement. Her tenure in the advisors' association was finished. In fact, she was no longer even a member.

However, Mary was not one to feel sorry for herself. She knew she still had a great reputation and was highly regarded in the industry. So she began a systematic process of letting key people know that she was available and open to opportunities to use her experience to help others. Here is what happened:

The President of the advisor association she once led asked her to head up a task force on how to help advisors with their succession planning to ensure a continued flow of new advisors into the industry. Given her own recent experience, Mary certainly had ideas about the right and wrong way to approach retirement.

Her former company offered to promote and subsidize a program wherein Mary would coach advisors on how to build and manage their practices. The opportunity to "give back" and help advisors succeed in their business had always been an important part of Mary's career.

The federal government invited her to be part of a national committee promoting financial literacy. Mary found this assignment particularly appealing. She knew from her experience as an advisor that the better educated people were about financial matters, the more likely they were to achieve financial success.

By the end of her first year of "retirement," Mary was as fully engaged in the industry as she wanted to be. She was energized and excited and making a valuable contribution. Above all, she was demonstrating that you should not retire "from" something until you have something to retire "to"!

Coach's Recap

- There is a continuum of financial capacity to retire that ranges from low to medium to high.

- On the low end, we find advisors with extreme lifestyle practices whose personal economic viability depends entirely on how well their business is doing. These advisors are usually counting on the sale of their business to fund their retirement.

- These advisors are also often the ones least prepared *emotionally* to exit the business because they know their own retirement picture isn't promising.

- At the other end of the spectrum are those advisors who are well prepared financially to retire. They typically have substantial personal assets outside their business, so they do not need to sell their practices to maintain their lifestyle in retirement.

- For many of those advisors, what happens to their clients is more important than the money.

- Advisors at this end of the continuum are also often the most prepared *emotionally* to transition out of their business as well.

- There is also a continuum of emotional readiness to retire that ranges from low to medium to high.

- On the low end of the scale are those advisors who are totally defined by their business. Their business is their life, and their life is their business, so they have no idea what else they would do with their time.

- They enjoy the "perks" of being their own boss and are driven by the recognition they receive for their work. They feel they could not survive without the business and vice versa.

- At the other end of the spectrum are those advisors who are ready to make the transition. They are very proud of what they have accomplished, but they have some other passion they would like to pursue.

- These advisors often want to share their knowledge or "give back" to the industry by coaching or mentoring someone.

- For a transition to be truly successful, advisors have to score well on both measures.

- Combining the two dimensions of "Financial Freedom" and "Emotional Enthusiasm" creates the Financial/Emotional Matrix with four quadrants:
  - Low Emotional + Low Financial
  - High Emotional + Low Financial
  - Low Emotional + High Financial
  - High Emotional + High Financial

My Succession Plan

Exercise #4 - Assessing My Readiness

1. **Assess your *financial freedom* to retire from your practice by completing the exercise below.** (Check all that apply)

    Low
    - ☐ I have little or no investments outside my business
    - ☐ My lifestyle depends entirely on how well my practice is doing
    - ☐ My business pays a lot of my personal expenses
    - ☐ I am counting on my business to fund my retirement

    Medium
    - ☐ I have personal assets to supplement proceeds from selling my practice
    - ☐ My practice pays me more than enough to support my lifestyle
    - ☐ My financial obligations are not onerous
    - ☐ The sale of my business will fund a large part of my retirement

    High
    - ☐ I have substantial personal assets outside the business
    - ☐ I do not need to sell my practice to maintain my lifestyle
    - ☐ What happens to my clients is more important than the money
    - ☐ I would like to coach or mentor someone into my business

2. **Overall, I would rate my *financial freedom* to transition out of my business as**
    - ☐ Low ☐ Medium ☐ High

3. **Assess your emotional enthusiasm to retire from your practice by completing the exercise below.** (Check all that apply)

    Low
    - ☐ I am totally defined by my business
    - ☐ I have no idea what to do next
    - ☐ The business couldn't run without me
    - ☐ I could not live without the "perks" and recognition

Medium

- ☐ My life extends beyond my practice
- ☐ I would like more time to pursue other interests
- ☐ I have a good team to support the business
- ☐ I am content with what I have accomplished and the fun I have had

High

- ☐ I cannot wait to get out of this business!
- ☐ I have a real passion I would like to pursue
- ☐ I am very proud of what I have accomplished
- ☐ I would like to coach/mentor someone to carry on in my place

4. **Overall, I would rate my *emotional enthusiasm* to transition out of my business as**

   ☐ Low ☐ Medium ☐ High

5. **The most accurate description of my readiness to transition from my business is:**

   a. ☐ Low Financial + Low Emotional

   b. ☐ Low Financial + High Emotional

   c. ☐ High Financial + Low Emotional

   d. ☐ High Financial + High Emotional

6. **Place an "X" on the spot on the matrix below that best illustrates your *financial freedom* and *emotional enthusiasm* to transition from your business.**

Financial/Emotional Matrix

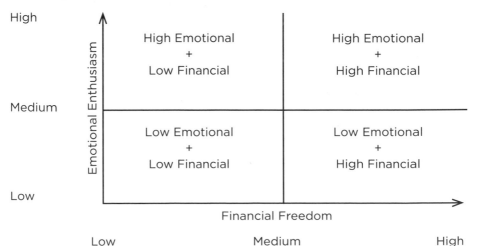

"I always worked until I had something done, and I always stopped when I knew what was going to happen next."
Ernest Hemingway

Chapter 5

When is the right time?

I had a couple more concepts I wanted to discuss with Henry that day, so when we returned with re-filled coffee cups, I started right back in.

"So, my little drawing is useful in visualizing where you are on your journey to retirement readiness?" I asked.

"It is," Henry said thoughtfully. "It also gives me perspective on what I have to do — better define what 'being prepared' actually means to me while I continue to build the value of my practice."

"That's an important point you've just made," I acknowledged. "Defining when you'll be ready to retire doesn't have to mean identifying the day you'll walk out the door, never to return. You are an entrepreneur, and the truth is that very few entrepreneurs can abruptly walk away from their business. In fact, research shows that fewer and fewer people in general go from full-time work to full-time leisure when they retire. Increasingly, there is some period of transition in-between.

"Advisors are classic examples, and we'll talk more about this a little later on when we take a deeper look into the various exit options you might consider."

"Well, the good news," Henry responded, "is that I have lots of time between now and the day I retire to figure this all out."

That last statement was the perfect segue into where I wanted to take our conversation next, so I asked, "Oh, really, so you have some sort of date in mind?"

"Not exactly," Henry acknowledged, "but probably sometime in the next ten years."

"That's pretty vague," I observed. "How did you determine that ten years was your target?"

"Oh, there's no real magic to that number — it just seems like a reasonable timeline. I will have had 35 years in the business by then and will probably be ready for a change. Actually, I hope I will have already started to slow down somewhat before then. Perhaps I'll be 'in transition' by then, as you describe it."

"Perhaps you will," I agreed. "As I said, we'll explore the various options more fully later on, but right now, I'm concerned about the informality of how you set ten years, potentially, as your exit date. I'm afraid I can't let you get away with that vagueness — so I'm going to insist you get a little more specific."

"But you said earlier that I get to decide when I am ready," Henry objected, "and, based on this little exercise we've just done, I don't know when that day will come."

"I realize that, and I'm not asking you to circle a date on the calendar and say 'That's it,'" I responded. "What I want you to avoid, however, is what I call the 'rolling ten-year trap.'"

"And that is?" he asked.

"That's when an advisor tells me they intend to retire within the next ten years. Then, when I ask them a year later how their plan is going, they say the same thing — 'I plan to retire within the next ten years.' Then, another year later, they say the same thing all over again. That ten-year target just keeps getting pushed out further and further until, one day, they realize they've run out of time and done very little planning."

"But I just don't know," Henry protested. "In fact, if anything, now that we have partially redefined what I think I want my transition out of the business to look like, I am probably less certain of when that will be. Even if I did set a date, I may well change my mind again!"

"And you never want to lose that prerogative," I added. "So nothing you decide today has to be chiseled in stone. If you develop new insights into yourself or the business and want to move the date forward or backward, you should feel free to do so. It's your life, so as I have said several times, you get to decide when and how.

"But as the old saying goes, 'A goal without a date is just a dream.' If you want to have structure around your decision-making and motivation to actually reach the retirement nirvana you want, you have to set a meaningful target date."

"OK Coach," Henry challenged, "what's a meaningful target date for me?"

"Actually," I answered, "I'm going to suggest you set two dates — not one."

"Two?" Henry reacted with some frustration in his voice.

"Yes. The first I refer to as the *'earliest possible date'* and the second is the *'latest acceptable date.'* Let me explain the difference and why both are important.

"The earliest possible date is, just as it suggests, the shortest interval of time before you'd even *consider* transitioning out of your business. It does not mean you will target that date or that you will do anything when it arrives. It is there just to help frame your timeline. In most cases, the big factor in determining this date is your progress towards having the financial freedom to choose.

"This date is the one by which you feel you will have the minimum amount of money or assets on which you'd be willing to retire. It is not the date by which you think you will have the financial strength to enjoy the full retirement lifestyle you want — just the date by which you would be able to retire if you chose to. Obviously, there is some emotional aspect to this as well that has to be satisfied by that date.

"It's like me telling a client, 'Yes, you could retire by this date, but it won't be the lifestyle you'd planned,'" Henry volunteered.

"There you go again — taking what I said in three paragraphs and condensing it to one sentence!"

"I sometimes feel coaches must think they get paid by the word," Henry joked, obviously in a better mood.

"You could be right!" I laughed. "So let me see if I can be more concise as we consider the second date — the latest acceptable.

"While being prepared financially will still be an issue, this date is driven more by your emotional enthusiasm to exit. It represents the date furthest out from today when you would be ready to transition. By this time, you will not want to wait any longer to pursue your post-retirement dreams, to spend more time with your family, to enjoy your hobbies, or, perhaps, because you feel you will not have the physical energy or motivation to continue managing your business.

"Another thing to think about in setting this date is the marketability of your practice. The longer you wait, the older your clients become, and unless you continue to add new, younger clients, you will eventually reach a point where revenue starts to decline. Investment clients will be drawing down on their assets for income or transferring them to their children, either voluntarily or through their wills. Insurance clients will become uninsurable. Financial planning clients will have less and less to plan.

"All other things being equal, buyers will pay substantially more for a practice with an average client age of 60 than one with an average age of 80."

"It's sort of like fine wine," Henry offered. "If you store it properly, it gets better and better over time — to a point. Then it starts to deteriorate because it's too old."

"That's a perfect analogy," I said, "and what makes it even more relevant is the fact that fine wine can continue to mature over a ten or even twenty-year period, but it can fade to being unpalatable very quickly if it's left too long past its peak. Just like an advisory practice!"

"OK, I'm beginning to see the value in setting these two dates," Henry conceded. "As you said before, we don't have to chisel them in stone, but they should be somewhat realistic."

"So what's your thinking?" I pressed him. "Knowing your financial position today and having some idea of what it could be at some point down the road, when is the earliest possible date you think you might be willing to consider transitioning out of your business?"

Henry sat staring straight ahead, for what seemed like a long time until he finally said, "Five years." Then, after a very brief pause, he continued, "And the answer to your next question is ten years. My earliest possible date is five years from now, and the latest acceptable is ten years. Is that OK with you?"

"It's entirely your choice, Henry, but if you are asking for my opinion, I think that is a very reasonable timeframe. Five years will give you the opportunity to increase the value of your practice, to better define what your transition will look like, and to become more emotionally prepared. Ten years out, barring anything unforeseen, you will be even more financially able, emotionally willing, and still young enough to give energy to whatever you decide to do next in your life.

"My guess is that your actual date will be somewhere in-between as you become increasingly clear about how you define your personal retirement. For now, we have a timeline within which to work, meaning we can set up milestones along the way against which we can measure your progress. You will be in complete control. How does that feel?"

"Good," said Henry. "It feels really good to have this settled."

"There's still lots of work to be done," I cautioned, "but putting those two stakes in the ground, so to speak, gives us the 'when' of your transition. Our next step is to determine the 'how.' There are lots of exit options available to you. We will want to try to narrow them down to those that come closest to meeting all your objectives.

"We've made significant progress in your transition planning today, Henry, so I suggest we break for now and come back at this in a week or so, after everything we've agreed upon has sunk in. Are you OK with that?"

"Sure thing," he replied, but once again, I could tell that his thoughts were far away, building a picture in his mind of what his world might look like going forward.

I was surprised when I walked back into Henry's boardroom a week later for our next session to see that my hand-drawn diagram of the Financial/Emotional Matrix from our last get-together was still up on the whiteboard. What's more, someone had even colored in the quadrants the way I had suggested:

Financial/Emotional Matrix[1]

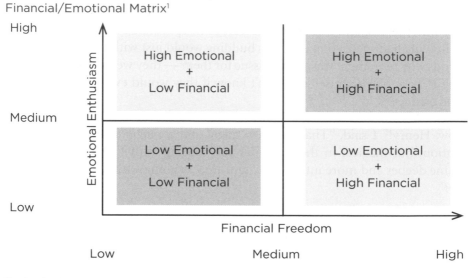

"What's this, Henry?" I asked. "Kids have been playing?"

"No," he laughed. "It was me! Shortly after our last meeting, I had a business-owner client and his wife in here for their annual review, and I had forgotten to erase your handiwork. I did not want them to feel I was hiding some great secret from them, so I just left it there. It turned out to be a great move.

"They have been investment clients for quite a while, and although we've always talked about their eventual retirement as one element of their plan, I know they have never been fully engaged in that part of the discussion. Their vision of retirement was to pass the family business they jointly owned down to their children someday. They didn't really know when that might be or how it would be done or if they could count on any money from it, so it didn't figure prominently in our work together. We focused on accumulating as much capital as we could outside the business.

"Well, when the wife saw your drawing, she asked what it was all about. I was about to dismiss it as unimportant, politely of course, when it struck me that the conversations you and I have been having could easily apply to these clients. So I did my best imitation of you and started explaining the need to be prepared

1   Derived from John Leonetti's book *Exiting Your Business, Protecting Your Wealth* www.pinnacleequitysolutions.com

both financially and emotionally for retirement. I found some colored pens and shaded each quadrant as I described it.

"The effect was magical! Suddenly, our conversation about their retirement went to a completely new level. They really opened up to me — about the capabilities of their children and their concern for the business if the kids were in charge. At one point, the husband was almost in tears as he speculated that the business he and his wife had spent so many years building would just wither away. It became obvious why retirement wasn't a big issue for them — they weren't sure they were going to have one because they didn't know if they would ever be able to let go of the business!"

"Wow, Henry!" I said, "That's both a tragic and a magic story. Tragic in the situation, but magical in the way your relationship with that client suddenly became deeper and more intimate. Where are you going with these people from here?"

"Aha!" Henry exclaimed. "That's the best part. I told them more about the conversations you and I have had and how you got me to think more clearly about what I wanted from my work and my life. I shared how important it was for me to have a plan to ensure my clients are well taken care of and that I retire on my own terms. I told them how you completed a formal valuation of my business and that we were going to work on a plan to maximize the value for the day I decide to transition out. They really liked the idea of a gradual transition from their business because it would allow them to see if their children were capable of continuing on in their stead."

"And if they weren't?" I interrupted. "What then?"

"That was another great moment because I asked the same question," Henry said proudly. "And for the first time in their lives, they talked about the possibility of selling their business rather than simply passing it to their children. I could tell it was a moral dilemma for them, but they realized that it opened up a whole new sphere of possibilities. I could actually feel their enthusiasm for retirement growing right here in this room. It was awesome!"

"Wow again, Henry!" I congratulated him. "You did a great job and a very good deed for those folks."

"Wait," he interjected. "The story isn't finished yet. I know you work exclusively with financial advisors — otherwise, I would have arranged for you to meet them, and I am sure they would have hired you on the spot. So I have volunteered to be their 'coach' — to work with them through their succession planning process. Obviously, I am a beginner at this, so I am going to have to cheat like mad. I am just going to follow what you do with me and apply it to their situation. I am pretty confident I can do that and add much more value to my role as their financial advisor. Am I crazy for wanting to do this?"

"No, you're not crazy, Henry," I responded. "In fact, I think it is a fabulous idea for several reasons. First, you will certainly help your clients sort out one of the most important issues in their lives — how to realize the value of the years of effort and risk-taking that went into building their business.

Second, in my experience, the teacher often learns more than the student does. Working through the process with your clients will bring insight and clarity to you with regard to your own exit strategy. That can only help us as you and I continue to develop your transition plan.

And finally, you'll gain enough confidence in the process and its value that you'll want to share it with more people than these clients you have described. I am willing to bet you have other business-owner clients who would be interested in your guidance as they contemplate their own succession. Right?"

"Of course! Many of my clients own small-to-medium sized businesses because, as you know from our previous work together, that was my primary target market. A lot of them are around my age — some older. I have tried to talk to them about including the value of their business in their investment plan, but the most common response has been 'No, Henry, my business is separate from my investments.' They don't seem to appreciate that a large part of their net worth is tied up in a single stock — their micro-cap, privately-held company — with all the risk that entails.

"If I could get them engaged in this process — where they had to think about being both financially and emotionally ready to leave their business — I think they would start to see how important it is for them to have a plan to someday monetize the value their business. Then we could truly do a good job of managing their wealth with proper asset allocation."

"And when they do exit their business, you can continue to manage their wealth, including proceeds from the sale of their business," I suggested.

"Yes!" Henry answered emphatically. "Even if I am already into my own transition plan, think what it would do to the value of my practice if a prospective buyer knew there were a significant number of clients who were planning on selling their businesses and investing the proceeds through our firm. The potential could be tens of millions of dollars of new assets to manage, just waiting to happen!"

"It's my turn to say 'Awesome!' Henry. It is a great deal for everyone. Your clients get advice they sorely need. Their lives become more assured. You set in motion the potential for a significant inflow of new investment assets to manage. The value of your business increases. It's win-win all around."

"What could be better than that?" Henry asked with a wide smile on his face.

"Actually," I answered, "there is another huge benefit that could come from this."

"And that is?"

"Recall from our last engagement how we talked about the need to periodically re-invent or re energize your business from time to time to take it to a new level?"

"Yes, I do," Henry responded enthusiastically, still on a high from his new business development idea. He jumped up, grabbed a pen, and started drawing on the whiteboard.

"This is the practice growth curve," he said as he drew a large "S" on the board. "It starts off slowly, builds momentum, and then begins to plateau as the business matures.

"In order to continue to grow, you have to start a new curve, like this."

"Where the two curves overlap is the zone of opportunity to re-invent the business to take it to the next level. The important thing is to start before the business begins to plateau. That's what we did, isn't it?"

I could tell that Henry was proud that he remembered and was very much enjoying the role reversal of being the teacher instead of the student.

"It is, and your business has come a very long way since then. I'm thinking it's time to do it again — probably for the last time before you exit."

"What do you have in mind?" he asked with a look that said 'Don't rain on my parade right now — I'm feeling good!'

"Your enthusiasm for succession planning has grown by leaps and bounds in a short period of time, to the point where you see tremendous business opportunity in becoming a coach for some of your clients. Could you also see attracting new clients who might be interested in that same advice and service?"

"Why not?" Henry exclaimed. "I am pretty sure I could also get referrals from some of my current clients to other business owners — their customers, suppliers, friends, and so on — possibly their clients' accountants and lawyers as well, using this approach rather than the standard 'I'm a great financial advisor.' There is huge potential."

"Then I suggest we use business-owner succession planning as the basis on which to re-define your business and take it to new heights between now and the date you ultimately decide to transition out yourself. It could become the theme of your marketing and referral messaging and the focus of your work until then.

"I am not saying you should abandon everything you are doing now to build and maintain your practice, but I believe adding this specialty to your list of capabilities and services will re-energize you and invigorate your business. You will not only be working to maximize the value of your practice for its eventual sale, you will be doing something new, exciting, and very valuable to others. Does that appeal to you?"

"It certainly does!"

"This also plays into your decisions around the 'earliest possible' and 'latest acceptable' transition dates for you. If this really takes off, you might reach the first date sooner because you will be better prepared financially. On the other hand, you might stretch the later date out a bit if you are having lots of fun and feel you are really helping others with their own retirement plans."

"I like it a lot," Henry offered. "My only concern is making sure I am actually sufficiently well-informed to be able to provide good advice. You have been doing this for a long time, so it is easy for you. Don't I have a lot to learn first?"

"Of course, there is specific knowledge I've gained over the years that helps me understand the world of a financial advisor pretty well — which is one of the reasons I restrict my coaching practice to our industry. However, many of the issues around business-owner succession are universal — they apply to every entrepreneur. There are also courses you can take, such as the Certified Business Exit Consultants™ program offered by John Leonetti's Pinnacle Equity Solutions[1]. I will send you some information on it.

"Importantly, as I think you have discovered, a large part of this has to do with the emotional aspects of succession rather than the technical ones. Dealing with clients' emotions is something you do every day. You are skilled at asking questions, listening, and incorporating what your clients say into your recommendations. This type of work is no different. As you know, you do not have to be a plumber to help a plumbing contractor with their retirement plans. Nor do you have to be a plumbing contractor to help one with their succession plan."

"OK," Henry said, "I'm in and ready to go! What's my next lesson, Teach?"

I was thrilled with how this session had gone. Not only had we advanced Henry's plan for his own transition, we had also found a new inspiration for his business — one that would take his business to a higher level and thereby enhance its value upon his retirement.

Most important to me was the fact that Henry had come up with the idea himself. There is nothing more rewarding for a coach than to have a client take something you have said or done and elevate it to a new level through their own insight and passion. I had intentionally left my drawing on the whiteboard in Henry's boardroom in hopes that he might look at it again as a reminder of what we had discussed. I never dreamed it would become a catalyst for the next stage of his career and his life.

---

1 www.pinnacleequitysolutions.com

Another Illustrative Case in Point

Waiting Too Long

Antonio first thought about selling his practice ten years ago. He had received an unsolicited offer that brought the value of the business he had built into focus for the first time. He engaged our firm to complete a formal valuation to confirm that the offer was a fair one. While our valuation came in slightly above the purchaser's, it was close enough for Antonio to enter into a "lock-up" agreement and formal due-diligence process.

The process took several months; however, as the completion date got closer and closer, Antonio decided the deal "just didn't feel right," so he terminated the negotiation and went back to building and managing his business.

By the time five more years passed, several other suitors had approached Antonio about merging or buying his business, and while he always listened to their proposals, each time he told them, "The time just isn't right for me." Stock markets had been rising at an above-average pace for several years, and Antonio's assets under management were growing exponentially, along with his income.

The accelerating stock market performance led to a feeding frenzy for good books of business as advisors sought to capture more clients and assets in the most expeditious way — through acquisitions. Multiples being offered sometimes seemed irrational as buyers competed for the attention of potential sellers.

By now, Antonio's business was of sufficient size that he was picked up on the radar of a major bank-owned firm which was aggressively pursuing large books of business. They approached him with an all-cash offer that was considerably higher than anything Antonio had seen before. He once again engaged our firm to do a formal valuation, and we confirmed that the offer was, indeed, at the upper end of any valuation range.

Whether it was greed or an appetite to "roll the dice one more time," Antonio rejected the offer, stating that he believed his business would increase in value by another 50% within two years. He felt he would always have the opportunity to go back to the bank-owned firm and sell his business to them for a much higher price.

Twelve months later, stock markets around the world dropped cataclysmically in a rout that would last two years. Antonio's assets under management fell by more than 40% as stock values crashed and clients retreated to "safer" investments. The bank-owned firm had stopped buying practices, and the only offers Antonio received were from opportunistic buyers looking for bargain prices from distressed sellers.

The good news is that Antonio didn't quit. He knew he had a solid foundation under his business, so he set to work re-building his practice. It took almost three years, but Antonio did manage to bring his assets back close to the level they had been prior to the market meltdown.

Unfortunately, the stress and effort took its toll on him, both physically and emotionally. For the third time, Antonio asked us to do a valuation of his business because he was finally ready to sell. This time, our analysis suggested a price range that was approximately 30% less than the all-cash offer the bank-owner firm had made more than five years previously.

Antonio accepted the first reasonable offer that came along and retired from the business — deflated, disillusioned, and disappointed.

Coach's Recap

- Defining when you will be ready to retire does not have to mean identifying the day you *will* walk out the door, never to return. The truth is that very few entrepreneurs can abruptly walk away from their business. More often, there is some period of transition in-between.

- You must avoid the 'rolling ten-year trap.' That is where an advisor says they intend to retire within the next ten years. Then, when asked a year later how their plan is going, they say the same thing — "I plan to retire within the next ten years." Then, another year later, they say the same thing. That ten-year target keeps getting pushed out until, one day, they have run out of time and done very little planning.

- You should set two dates: "*earliest possible*" and "*latest acceptable.*"

- Your "earliest possible date" is the date by which you will have the minimum financial capability to retire. You may not have the financial freedom to enjoy the full retirement lifestyle you want — but it is the date by which you'd be able to retire, if you chose to.

- Your "*latest acceptable date*" represents the date furthest out from today when you would be ready to transition. By this time, you will not want to wait any longer to pursue your post-retirement dreams.

- You must also consider the marketability of your practice. The longer you wait, the older your clients become and the less valuable your practice is to a potential purchaser. All other things being equal, buyers will pay substantially more for a practice with an average client age of 60 than one with an average age of 80.

- Many advisors use the lessons they have learned through their own succession planning to counsel business-owner clients. In fact, they often build substantial practices around providing this service.

- This approach has a number of benefits:
  - It helps clients monetize the value of the years of effort and risk-taking that went into building their business.
  - Working through the process with clients brings insight and clarity to your own exit strategy.
  - It builds enough confidence in the process and its value to share it with business-owner clients who would be interested in your guidance as they contemplate their own succession.

- You can use business-owner succession planning as the basis on which to re-define your business and take it to new heights between now and the date you transition out yourself. It could become the theme of your marketing and referral messaging and the focus of your work until then.

- Adding this specialty to your list of capabilities and services will re-energize you and invigorate your business. You will not only be working to maximize the value of your practice for its eventual sale, you will be doing something new, exciting, and very valuable to others.

- Dealing with clients' emotions is something you do every day. You are skilled at asking questions, listening, and incorporating what your clients say into your recommendations. Counselling clients on their own succession plan is no different.

My Succession Plan

Exercise #5 – Getting the Timing Right

1. **Regarding the target date for my transition/succession:**

    a. The earliest possible target date for my transition/succession is

    _____

    b. The latest acceptable target date for my transition/succession is

    _____

2. **I would describe my transition as a period when I will:**
    (Choose most applicable)

    ☐   Slow down

    What does that mean? _____

    ☐   Maintain a steady pace

    What does that mean? _____

    ☐   Accelerate my business

    What does that mean? _____

3. **If you chose "Accelerate my business" above, how do you intend to do that?** (Check all that apply)

    ☐   Increase my marketing

    How? _____

    ☐   Develop a new market

    Which market? _____

    ☐   Offer new products and/or services

    What products/services? _____

    ☐   Hire additional staff

    For what role(s)? _____

    ☐   Change my pricing

    To what? _____

    ☐   Work "harder"

    How? _____

    ☐   Other (Specify) _____

    What? How? _____

"I always wonder why birds stay in the same place when they can go anywhere on earth. Then I ask myself the same question."
Harun Yahya

Chapter 6

What is the best exit option?

"As I said earlier, Henry, we now have an idea of the 'when' of your transition — sometime in the next five to ten years. And we have just added some great thoughts about how your business might progress between now and then — with a focus on providing advice to business owners around their own succession planning.

"The next step is to look at 'how' your exit is going to play out. Because you want to use the conversations we have as the basis for your work with clients, I think we should walk through all the options — even though, based on our discussions so far, several of them will not apply to you. However, you will probably want to be aware of the full range of choices so you will be familiar with the options for any client situation you encounter. Does that work for you?"

"Sure does," Henry offered, sounding a bit like someone who suddenly realized they knew a lot more about a subject than they thought they did.

I went to the whiteboard to write.

Option #1 – Do nothing

"In the broadest sense," I began, "there are five exit options that I have seen being played out by financial advisors. The first one is not so much an option as the lack of one — and that is to do nothing. In other words, this is the default chosen by advisors who do not have or intend to have a succession plan. They are simply going to continue with their businesses and their lives as if they were immortal. Essentially, what they are saying is, 'I'll just keep working until I drop, and after that, I don't really care what happens to my business.'

"I suspect these people may have quite sad lives to begin with — given that they don't seem to care about themselves or their clients. However, I have to say that I am surprised by the number of advisors who tell me they have no interest in a succession plan because they never intend to retire. Therefore, I have to assume this is the option they have chosen.

"Or, as we talked about earlier, they have a severe case of 'lifestyle practice' and can't afford to retire," Henry offered.

"You're right, Henry. That is a very real possibility — and one few would be willing to admit, I am sure."

Option #2 - Carry on

"That brings me to the second option, which isn't all that different from 'doing nothing.' This is the one where the advisor simply says, 'I am going to continue on with my business until I decide one day to stop. There will be lots of buyers around, so I'll just sell to the highest bidder at that time.' Again, not much regard for the clients here and no certainty around timing of the advisor's exit or transition.

"That uncertainty can play on the minds of clients, who will want to know what plans the advisor has in place for their personal retirement and how they will continue to be served. In these situations, it is not unusual to see a gradual defection of clients to other advisors and a corresponding systematic decline in revenue. For sure, referrals will be few and far between because clients and centers of influence are unlikely to refer others to an advisor whose future plans for their business are so ambiguous."

"And won't potential buyers be looking for a bargain, knowing that the advisor is going to sell no matter what?" Henry asked.

"True, again, Henry," I said with a small chuckle to myself at how his interest in the nuances of succession planning was starting to blossom.

"However, there is an interesting paradox in this approach in that, although it calls for the least amount of advance planning next to doing nothing, it may actually turn out to be the best method for maximizing payout to the advisor!"

"I don't see that," Henry challenged.

"It relates to the point you made earlier about lifestyle practices and not being able to afford retirement. For a large number of advisors, they are better off to 'run out' their business for a few years than sell it outright. In the end, they will receive more money overall."

"How so," Henry asked, "given what you said earlier about clients leaving and referrals drying up?"

"Because it is a seller's market right now, almost any book of business can be sold, let's say, for one to two times net revenue. So an outright sale might yield the advisor up to two years of retirement income at their current lifestyle.

"But what if, instead, the advisor continued to run their practice, even though the revenue was steadily declining due to client defections. Over the next three to five years, they would likely earn more than the sale price, depending on the pace of defections, market conditions, and so on. And they would still have the option of continuing to receive a declining income or sell what's left to someone who was just looking to add clients to their practice no matter what they looked like.

"It is not all that unusual for me to suggest to some advisors whose lifestyle practices won't fetch much in the marketplace to just 'let it ride' because they'll end up overall with more money in their jeans. While that approach will not do much for client confidence, it has the advantage of enabling advisors who have no idea of what they will do in retirement to keep their hand in the game as long as they want. They can also gradually adjust their way of life to align with their diminishing income."

"Not the ideal scenario," Henry observed, "but probably better than running out of money entirely in one or two years."

"You are right," I continued, "but let's move on to one of the most popular retirement scenarios advisors tell me they are going to pursue."

"I'd think just about anything would be better than the first two," Henry offered.

"I said the next one was popular. I didn't say it was necessarily good!" I joked.

Option #3 – Partial withdrawal

"Under this option, the advisor decides he or she is going to remain in the business, but 'scale back my involvement.' What they usually mean by that is they are going to work only with a small group of clients — and, predictably, they are the practice's 'best' clients. They intend then to either sell the rest of their book or bring someone in to run it."

"I've heard a number of advisors in my dealer firm say that's what they intend to do," Henry said, "and I have to admit, it has appeal."

"Of course, it does," I agreed. "Less responsibility, fewer hours on the job, spending most of your time with people you like and who like you, probably with minimum service requirements, without having to give up many of the rewards and perks you enjoy as an advisor — what's not to like?"

"So what's the problem?" Henry asked.

"The problem is the old '80/20 rule,' which suggests that, in a typical financial advisory practice, 80% of the revenue comes from 20% of the clients. And guess which clients these advisors want to keep as they transition to a lower level of involvement?"

"The 20% who are generating 80% of the revenue, obviously," Henry responded immediately.

"And where does that leave whoever is taking over the business?" I asked.

"Looking after 80% of the clients for 20% of the revenue," Henry said, knowing where the conversation was heading.

"That's not only a bad situation from a workload and reward perspective for the successor, but also from a valuation point of view," I suggested.

"That's pretty obvious," Henry offered. "If the revenue drops by 80%, so does the value of the business."

"Actually," I came back, "it is worse than that. Recall that the value of an advisor's practice is determined by its future profitability. Our research shows that not only do a relatively small number of top clients contribute most of the revenue to the business, they also account for 100% of its *profitability*! Take away the revenue from those clients, and the rest of the business will likely operate at a loss. No profit equals no value."

"So the advisor who thinks they are going to keep, say, the top 20–30 clients and sell the rest of their practice has really ripped all the value out of the business," Henry concluded.

"Absolutely," I agreed, happy again that Henry was coming to his own realizations about the key considerations in succession planning.

I continued, "But that doesn't necessarily make this option a bad choice, which is why it is the preferred option for many advisors for the reasons we stated — keeping active with less responsibility, spending time only with people you like, minimum service requirements, and so on.

"My primary caution to advisors considering this option, however, is not to count on selling what's left of their practice after they strip out the best clients for too high a price. I have seen, for example, advisors who have a practice valued at $1 million think that if they only keep 20% of the clients, they can sell the rest of their book for $800,000. It simply isn't going to happen that way if potential buyers have any common sense at all."

"It's the old 'can't have your cake and eat it too' scenario, isn't it?" Henry noted.

"That it is," I said reflectively. "And on that tasty note, I'd like another coffee."

"OK," Henry started back in as soon as we returned to the boardroom. He was really getting wound up by our discussions. "By way of review, the first option is not really an option but more of a default, and that is to do nothing. No succession plan required.

"The second option is slightly better in that you intend to someday exit the business, but you are not going to do any advance planning. When you decide it's time to 'hang up your spurs,' so to speak, you'll just look for a buyer, do a deal, and retire. Again, no succession plan needed.

"With both of these options, you run the risk of client defection and reduction in referrals as clients and centers of influence become increasingly concerned about the uncertainty around you being there."

"The third option," Henry continued, "is a partial withdrawal, where the advisor retains a small number of key clients and either brings someone in to manage the rest or sells that part of the client base."

"You've got the option right, and I hate to be a nit-picker when you are getting so caught up in the opportunity of advising your clients on their own succession, but I feel compelled to make a point."

"Yes?" Henry said a bit defensively.

"Our industry is different from many others because of the deep and intimate relationships you have with your clients. Furthermore, your revenue is very much dependent on maintaining those relationships through ongoing service, periodic reviews, regular communication, etc.

"Another key difference is that many business owners have something tangible to sell when they decide to retire — a physical building, inventory, machinery and equipment, a patented process, long-term contracts, and the like.

"The only thing advisors have to transition to someone else are their client relationships. In that sense, advisors cannot really 'sell' their client base because they cannot sell people. As we have discussed, what an advisor sells, so to speak, is the revenue expected from continuing those client relationships. I apologize for going on a bit about this, but when I hear advisors say they are going to 'sell' their clients, it raises my hackles a bit."

"Fair enough," Henry conceded. So back to the third option — keep the top client *relationships* and transition the rest of the *relationships*," Henry said with emphasis on the word to show he understood.

"The advantages of this option include keeping your hand in the game for a while and continuing to enjoy ongoing revenue from people with whom you like to spend time. The disadvantage is that you likely strip all the profitability out of the rest of the practice, which may make it unsaleable, or at least worth much less down the road. It will also be more difficult to find a good successor. If there is good news in this approach, it is that there has to be some pre-planning and diligence around finding a successor. Does that about describe it?"

"Excellent summation, Professor!" I joked again.

Option #4 – Internal Transition

"And that brings us to the fourth option, which is in many ways the one that looks like the best choice for everyone involved, on paper at least. I am referring to an outright transition or sale to an 'insider.'"

"With an 'insider' being defined as…?" Henry interrupted.

"An associate or associates working within your current practice or, at least, within your dealer firm. That would also include family members, although there are special considerations for family members that we'll talk about later.

"Internal transitions, as they are also often called, have several advantages. First, they are the least disruptive to clients — no paperwork to complete, no new firm to evaluate — ideally, it's 'business as usual.'

"Secondly, it gives the exiting advisor the best view of their prospective successor candidate. Certainly, if they are already working in your practice, you will have seen them in action, know how they work and deal with clients, and understand their philosophies with respect to products and planning, etc. If they are not part of your practice, but within the same firm, you will likely know them by reputation or through meetings at company conferences and so on. You will also have the ability to quiz Head Office personnel, especially the Compliance Department, about their practices and regard for company policies.

"You will often find this arrangement used in situations where there are senior staff members who are interested in acquiring the business through a 'management buyout.'"

"Like in my brother's case," Henry jumped in. "He sold his business to a group of senior employees."

"Exactly," I said. "And there are lots of ways that can be accomplished, for example, through employee stock option plans, if the business is large enough. For the majority of financial advisors, however, the more likely scenario for an internal transfer is a sale to one or two associates within their own firm."

"So minimizing disruption to clients and familiarity with your successor are two very good reasons for pursuing this option," Henry concluded. "In addition, it has to be good for the dealer firm to have a smooth internal transition rather than losing clients to a competitor. So everyone is a winner, as you said. Any other advantages?"

"Yes, many dealer firms today have corporate-sponsored programs to encourage internal transitions. The largest component of them is normally some assistance with financing the transaction; however, they could include administrative support, client communication, and other resources to make the transfer of clients from one advisor to another as easy as possible."

"Any downside?" Henry asked.

"There could be. The most common obstacle advisors tell me they encounter with respect to internal transitions is the lack of a suitable successor. In a smaller firm, there would simply be fewer internal candidates. Even in larger firms, if the exiting advisor has some pretty definitive ideas about the type of person they want to carry on their business and be custodian of their legacy, they may not think there is anyone qualified within their current practice or within their dealer firm, at least not locally."

"That one strikes a bit close to home for me," Henry said slowly. "I'd have to think carefully about whom I'd want to take over and where they might come from. There isn't anyone within my firm who immediately jumps out to me as being the ideal candidate."

"We'll fully explore the whole topic of who is a suitable candidate as soon as we finish looking at all the exit options," I promised. "For now, let's finish this discussion by noting that there are a couple of other, more practical things that might get in the way of this being the best option for an advisor."

"Such as?" Henry asked, but I could tell he was still thinking about our last point of discussion.

"In some situations, where it is contractually spelled out that clients are clients of the firm and not the advisor, an advisor may simply be prohibited from transitioning their clients to someone else of their own choosing. The firm, itself, may have a program to acquire the accounts and redistribute them to an advisor or group of advisors they favor or who are 'next in line.' Hopefully, in these circumstances, there is fair compensation to the exiting advisor — but I have to tell you that is not always the case.

"This brings me to another instance in which the exiting advisor often has limitations: where the firm is participating in the financing, and they have mandatory valuation formula in place that restricts the ability of the departing advisor to negotiate the transfer price."

"That assumes all 'practices are equal' — which, as we have already discussed, they are not," Henry said with some emphasis. Again, I smiled a little to see that more of our earlier conversations had stuck with him than I might have initially thought.

Option #5 - External Sale

"That's a perfect segue to the final exit option — an external sale — to someone outside your firm. That may be a direct competitor, an industry consolidator, or, if the practice is sufficiently large and profitable, an institution or private equity firm.

"While this is a popular topic of conversation among advisors, I have to say that it is not the most common succession strategy actually used in our industry. That being said, I can see it being an appealing choice for some of your business-owner clients as you help them with their retirement planning."

"The pluses and minuses?" Henry asked.

"Well, on the plus side, it opens up the whole market as you seek the best successor. If there is no suitable candidate internally, you can dramatically expand your search area to find the right person to carry on in your stead.

"Financially, it is also the option under which you are likely to get the best price. In today's 'seller's market' for practices, once the word is out that there is a good book of business, or even a not-so-good one, for sale, potential buyers will beat a path to the seller's door. They can expect several bids and increased multiples as a result of the competition."

"Hopefully, price isn't the only consideration," Henry pleaded.

"I agree that it shouldn't be, and we'll talk more about some of the other considerations, including choosing the right successor, soon. Still, we have to acknowledge that this option often leads to highest price."

"But the downside is that this is the most disruptive to the clients," Henry asserted. "Paperwork, change of routine, change in reporting, change in culture, for example, from a small, independent practice to a large financial institution — these things will affect the client far more than the departing advisor."

"True, in most cases," I agreed. "On the other hand, I have seen situations where a change to a competitor firm brought new services and capabilities to clients they didn't previously have.

"We should also note that selling to an outsider brings a lot more work with it to complete proper due diligence on someone you don't know."

"Just to complete my list, then," Henry said, "let me summarize the last two exit options as either *internal* or *external* transitions. The first has the advantage of being easiest on the clients and, often, easiest on the advisor — provided you have a good candidate 'on the inside.' On the other hand, an external sale will likely result in a better price but is far more disruptive for everyone. In some firms, it may not even be an option due to contract restrictions. Is that a good synopsis?"

"An excellent one!" I congratulated Henry. "Now if only the process of choosing the right exit option was as clear as your summary."

Another Illustrative Case in Point

Life Happens

Ralph and Randy had been working in the same independent dealer firm for more than ten years. While they never considered themselves 'best friends,' they certainly respected each other and used to meet two or three times a year at company or industry events. Those encounters often ended with long conversations over late-night cocktails about how challenging it was becoming to run a profitable practice.

When the market meltdown of 2008-09 occurred, both felt the financial pressure, and they agreed that combining their businesses into one location would save both of them money in rent, operating costs, and even salaries if they shared staff.

It was not Ralph and Randy's intention to work as 'partners' in the true sense of the word, since each wanted to run their own book of business and be responsible for their own business development. They agreed to split all costs 50/50, although there were times when they each quietly felt they were paying more than their share, depending on who was using most of the staff time, etc.

While they did not have a formal written agreement with respect to the business, Ralph and Randy verbally agreed on a contingency plan in the event that one of them was unable to carry on their business, due to death or long-term disability. In that situation, the "survivor" would agree to buy the other's book of business at a "fair price."

Ralph was ten years older than Randy and, unfortunately, within 18 months of moving into the joint office, he began to experience health problems to the point where his doctor suggested that he should probably think about retiring from the business altogether within a year if he wanted to enjoy any retirement at all.

Based on their ability to work alongside each other and familiarity, Ralph assumed that Randy would be the obvious candidate to buy his business when he retired. Given the short time frame, he wanted to formalize an agreement as soon as possible.

When he broached the subject with Randy, however, he was shocked to find that Randy did not share his enthusiasm for buying his business. It was one thing, Randy said, to agree to assist with clients in the event of an emergency such as death or disability. Buying an entire practice all at once, however, was not part of the strategic plan he had for his business. Furthermore, he said, he did not really have the financial resources to pay Ralph, even though he wasn't sure what the price and terms might be.

Once he recovered from his initial disappointment, Ralph decided he was not going to take "No" for an answer quite so easily. He had observed Randy at work with his clients and how he treated the staff. He knew from their in-office discussions that he and Randy were philosophically aligned with respect to the importance of financial planning and helping clients meet their objectives within a risk level they could manage.

He also knew that many of his clients already thought Ralph and Randy were partners in the business and that they would readily accept Randy as their new advisor when Ralph retired. In short, a buy-sell agreement between the two of them would be the best possible outcome for Ralph and his clients. All he had to do was convince Randy.

So Ralph put together a presentation on the benefits to everyone — clients, staff, dealer firm, Randy himself, and Ralph's family — of a transition of Ralph's book of business to Randy. He detailed the process and timing and described how clients could be transferred with little disruption to them and limited resource strain on current staff. Importantly, he demonstrated how Randy could acquire the business for a relatively small down payment and finance the balance out of future cash flow from Ralph's clients.

His final appeal was for Randy to honor the spirit of their verbal agreement regarding death or disability because, in fact, it was in anticipation of those contingencies that Ralph was pushing for a deal.

By the time Ralph finished his presentation, Randy was on board with the proposal. The details were nailed down, and a formal Agreement of Purchase and Sale drawn up. The transaction closed six months later, and six months after that, Ralph retired.

Coach's Recap

There are five common exit options

- **#1 – Do nothing**
    - Not so much an option as the lack of one, this is the default chosen by the advisor who does not have or intend to have a succession plan.
    - They are simply going to continue with their business until circumstances force them to stop.
    - No succession plan is required.

- **#2 – Carry on**
    - The succession plan is simple — work until you no longer want to — sell what is left of the business at that time to whoever will pay the most.
    - The uncertainty can worry clients, who will want to know what plans the advisor has for how they will continue to be served.
    - This approach may lead to a gradual defection of clients and a systematic decline in revenue.
    - Referrals will suffer because clients and centers of influence are unlikely to refer others to an advisor whose plans are so ambiguous.
    - Potential buyers will be looking for a bargain price knowing the advisor is going to sell no matter what.
    - This may be the best approach for advisors whose lifestyle practices won't fetch much in the marketplace. They may well end up with more money overall than trying to sell their business outright.

- **#3 – Partial exit**
    - The advisor decides to remain in the business but scale back their involvement by working only with a small group of the practice's best clients. They intend to either sell the rest of their book or bring someone in to run it.
    - This option is appealing because it means less responsibility, fewer hours on the job, spending most of your time with people you like, and minimum service requirements, without having to give up many of the rewards and perks that come with being an advisor.
    - The problem is the "80/20 rule," which suggests that 80% of revenue comes from 20% of the clients. If the advisor keeps 20% of the clients who generate 80% of the revenue, that leaves whoever is taking over the business looking after 80% of the clients for 20% of the revenue.

- The actual outcome is worse than that since the value of an advisor's practice is determined by its future profitability. Research shows that not only do a small number of top clients contribute most of the revenue to the business, they also account for 100% of its *profitability*!
- Take away the revenue from those clients, and the rest of the business will likely operate at a loss. No profit equals no value.
- Advisors who keep the top 20–30 clients and sell the rest of their practice have really ripped all the value out of the business.

- #4 – Sale to an "insider"
  - Refers to transition or sale to an associate or associates working within your current practice or, at least, within your dealer firm. It also includes transitions to family members.
  - There are several advantages:

    - Least disruptive to clients

    - Gives the exiting advisor the best view of the prospective successor

    - Dealer firm may have corporate-sponsored programs to encourage internal transitions, including financing and administrative support, to make transfer as easy as possible
  - Downside could include:

    - Lack of a suitable internal successor

    - Contractual prohibition from transitioning clients to someone of the advisor's choosing

    - Firm may have a program to acquire the accounts and re-distribute them to an advisor they favor or who is "next in line"

    - If the firm is participating in the financing, they may have a mandatory valuation formula that restricts the ability of the departing advisor to negotiate the transfer price

- #5 – Sale to an "outsider"
  - Refers to a sale to someone outside your firm. That may be a direct competitor, an industry consolidator, or, if the practice is sufficiently large and profitable, an institution or private equity firm.
  - The advantages are:
    - Opens up the whole market for a successor if there is no suitable candidate internally
    - Likely to get the best price due to buyer competition
  - Downside is:
    - Most disruptive to the clients
    - A lot more work to complete proper due diligence on someone you don't know

My Succession Plan

Exercise #6 – Comparing Exit Options

1. <u>Based on what I know so far</u>, the exit option that appeals to me most is to:

   ☐ Carry on working as I am today

   Why? _____

   _____

   ☐ Carry on, while working to maximize value

   Why? _____

   _____

   ☐ Transition part of my business & continue to work the rest

   Why? _____

   _____

   ☐ Transition all of my business to an internal associate

   Why? _____

   _____

   ☐ Transition all of my business to a family member

   Why? _____

   _____

   ☐ Sell to a competitor

   Why? _____

   _____

   ☐ Other (Please specify)

   Why? _____

   _____

"It is in your moments of decision that your destiny is shaped."
Tony Robbins

Chapter 7

Which exit option is for me?

Due to scheduling demands on my part, a couple of weeks passed before Henry and I were able to get together again to continue our discussions regarding his succession plan. I started to apologize for the delay, but Henry waved me off that right away.

"Actually", he said, "I found the time very useful in thinking through some of our conversations and formulating a much clearer picture of the future I want to have in this business and afterwards."

"That's great," I responded. "Anything in particular jump out at you?"

"I guess the biggest thing is the seriousness of all this. I know I gave you a hard time when you first brought up the topic of retirement planning to me, and I was probably a bit gruff with you. However, I now realize just how important it is to make sure I am in control of my eventual transition from the business and that I make the right decisions. As you put it, it's my life's work and my legacy we are discussing here."

"Oh, Henry, I've seen you in far worse moods — especially on the golf course!" I couldn't help joking before getting serious. "But you got over any discontent very quickly and moved beyond my wildest dreams in how you not only saw the value in what we were talking about but enthusiastically embraced it as part of your business plan. A coach and advocate could not ask for more!

"What else did you think about?"

"I thought about all the assumptions we have to make and how even the best designed plan could come off the rails if something unexpected happened."

"Like what?"

"Like what if I become disabled or die or the markets crash again or my payout gets cut or the government changes the rules on us or clients decide they can do just as well with a robo-advisor or…"

"Whoa, Henry," I interjected, "you're making me dizzy with all this worry! Stop for a minute and listen to yourself. What would you say to a client who starts asking all those same questions — about their death or disability, about market volatility, about declining rates of return, about revised legislation or tax rules, or new technology?"

Henry calmed himself quite quickly and answered, "I'd tell them that is why we plan. No one knows the future for certain, so the best we can do is make decisions based on what we know today. If the world around us changes, we may have to change our minds about some things, but at least we will have the framework of a plan in place to guide us."

"And so…" I left the next statement to Henry to complete, confident he would easily see the parallel. He did.

"…our succession plan is built around how we feel the world will unfold from today's perspective. If we develop a different view, we may have to modify the plan."

"Feel any better?" I asked, somewhat sympathetically, but also a bit sarcastically.

"Yeah, sorry about that," Henry apologized. "It just seems like the more I learn about this, the more I realize how many decisions have to be made. That's probably why so many advisors put their succession plan off or ignore it altogether."

"This is also why so many of your clients are doing the same thing. You have a huge opportunity, both professionally and personally, to help them create a better future for themselves, those they care about and, perhaps, even society itself through their philanthropy. That is a pretty noble calling, don't you think?"

"It is for sure, and despite my concern about not having all the answers, I am getting more and more excited about the possibilities of working with clients on their succession plans."

"Then this might be a good time for me to show you a relatively simple way to help your clients narrow down their exit options. Interested?"

"Of course, fire away!"

"It goes all the way back to the Financial/Emotional Matrix that you've come to love and adore!" I began. "I see you finally erased it from your whiteboard, so let me quickly draw it again."

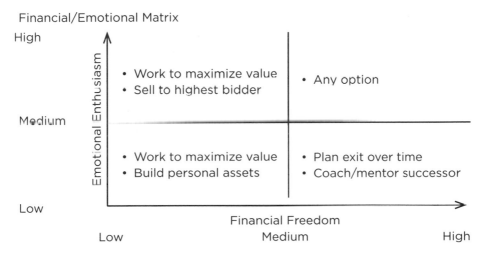

Financial/Emotional Matrix

"This time, however, instead of labelling the four quadrants as we did before, let's consider the exit options available within each. I will still speak in terms of the choices financial advisors have; however, you can think about the same options for your business-owner clients.

"For example, in the bottom left corner are advisors who have neither the financial freedom nor the emotional enthusiasm to retire. Their best option is dig in and work to maximize the value of their business. If they can increase their personal assets at the same time, all the better. As their overall financial capability expands, their emotional enthusiasm will also improve. The short-term objective is to move up or to the right. The longer-term goal is to advance both dimensions sufficiently to provide the freedom of choice."

"It kind of reminds me of Stephen Covey's 'Start with the end in mind'[1] approach," Henry added.

"Great observation, Henry! It is good advice at any time, but particularly when the journey is a long one.

1   Stephen Covey – The Seven Habits of Highly Effective People

"Let's move to the upper-left quadrant now. Here we find advisors who have a strong emotional desire to exit the business but limited financial capability. They, too, should work to maximize the value of their business in order to provide more financial freedom to choose when they exit the business. If the emotional desire to exit is very strong, because they have something else they really want to do or because they simply are not enjoying the business, they may want to sell to whoever will pay them the highest price.

"I have met a number of advisors who are in this position — they want to retire, perhaps due to age or health, but the value of their business and personal assets are insufficient to allow them the lifestyle they desire. Their plan then is to work for a few more years to improve their financial situation before they put their business on the market.

"I might argue there are other ways to approach this situation, such as forming a partnership with a younger advisor, but often, they simply want to continue doing what they have been doing for the shortest amount of time rather than make major changes in the way they operate."

"I can think of one or two of my clients who are in exactly that situation," Henry volunteered. "I can already imagine our first conversation about their succession plan — how much is enough, and how long do we have to achieve it before they just throw in the towel and sell to the highest bidder?"

"I am pretty sure you will find lots to talk about with a number of your clients very quickly," I observed.

"For example, if I were coaching an advisor who was in the bottom-right quadrant — well positioned financially but not yet ready emotionally — we would definitely work on a plan with a stated timeframe during which they could become more psychologically accepting of the notion of retiring. One thing that could help accomplish that is confidence in his or her successor. In that case, I might suggest we look for someone whom the founding advisor could coach or mentor."

"I can see how that would help," Henry agreed.

"Finally, of course, we have the top-right quadrant. Advisors who are fully there have the luxury of choice — they can stay as long as they wish and do whatever they feel is required to leave their business in the best shape possible."

"So it should be everyone's objective to move into the upper-right quadrant?"

"It should; however, the reality is that every advisor, or in your case, every business-owner client, is not going to be that patient. As we have talked about with respect to your own succession plan, you get to say when 'enough is enough, I'm ready.' I have always taken the position that we are seeking progress, not perfection, so my objective is to move people towards what they want. When they get close enough, they will tell me.

"This naturally leads me to asking, 'How close are you to articulating your personal transition plan?'"

"I think I am pretty close, but I still have a few questions, and that's what I hoped we could talk about today."

"Of course. Fire away with what you have so far. Start with the 'big rock' items like dates and exit options, if you have those developed in your mind."

"Actually, I do. Surprisingly, I found them to be easiest," Henry admitted.

"We've already talked about the timing — my 'earliest possible' date is five years from now and my 'latest acceptable' is ten years out."

"How did you arrive at that timeframe?" I asked.

"Pretty simple — the same way I do it for my clients. I projected the income that would be required to have the lifestyle I want down the road and then calculated my 'number' — the amount of capital I would need to generate that income over and above any capital I would like to use in another way, such as bequests to children, charity, and so on.

"Then I looked at the personal investments I have outside my business, along with my typical annual savings, and conservatively projected their total value year by year going forward. It was clear that they would not do the job alone unless I was willing to postpone my retirement until I was at least 80!

"Then I did the same exercise with my business — using the valuation you completed for me and projecting it ahead at a conservative rate on a year-by-year basis. I even threw in a market correction for safety! From there, I simply added the capital I could expect from my personal assets to the practice value each year until their total exceeded my 'number.' That happened around the fifth year; hence, my 'earliest possible' date of five years from now."

"A very reasoned and reasonable approach," I offered. "And if it turns out that your personal portfolio and/or business grow faster than anticipated, you can accelerate your 'earliest possible date.' That doesn't necessarily mean you will retire sooner — just that you'll have an earlier choice should you wish to exercise it.

"Similarly, if they grow more slowly, you can back off on your date. Again, you may not want to pull the trigger if your assets are not where you want them to be, but perhaps by that time, you may be willing to accept a slightly lesser lifestyle if circumstances dictate early retirement. Again, the choice will be all yours."

"I really like this whole notion of 'earliest possible' date," Henry volunteered enthusiastically. "It allows me to basically forget about retirement for the next five years. I can just put my head down and focus on getting ready for my transition, rather than ignoring or fretting about it."

"Excellent attitude! Now how about the other date — your 'latest acceptable'?"

"This one was harder, I admit. There are many more variables to be considered, so there is much more uncertainty around it. However, I decided on ten years for a number of reasons.

"First of all, I will have been in my business for 35 years by then. I think that is a good run. I have been well rewarded for my work, and I feel I have done a good job of setting my clients on the right path to their financial peace of mind. Give it another ten years from now, and I will start to see many of the plans I developed for clients begin to play out as they retire. I am confident most will be in at least as good a position as hoped — many will be far better off than originally anticipated. That will give *me* peace of mind.

"Secondly, I can see major changes coming to our industry — products, regulation, technology, client relationships, competition, compensation, etc. I have been able to adapt my practice to these developments as they occurred over the past 25 years, but I now have to accept that the rate of change is accelerating, and I believe that we will see an exponential transformation of the way we do business over the next five to ten years.

"I am not sure I will have the skill, energy, or desire to keep up for much more than that. I believe that what I have seen has been an *evolution* of my business, but it will become a *revolution* for advisors to manage in the future. I think it is going to take a younger person with a longer-term view to rise above these accelerating challenges and work them to advantage.

"My final point is that I am in good health today and am consciously trying to stay that way. However, I have to accept that, over time, we all take on a greater risk of disease or injury or general deterioration of our physical abilities. There are a lot of things I want to do when I retire, like travel, play more golf, volunteer with some charities. I don't want to postpone my retirement too long and increase the risk that I won't have the time, energy, and physical capability to do those things. Who knows, maybe I'll become a coach!"

"And I think you'd make a good one!" I offered before adding jokingly, "But then, you have had a great role model!"

"Whatever!" Henry shot back with a laugh.

"Seriously, Henry, as I think you know, I have a personal mission around bringing young people into the industry and helping them build great practices. If you ever feel a similar passion, I would encourage, endorse, and support you in any way I could. You definitely have the experience and the persona to influence others in a very positive way."

"Well, thanks for the vote of confidence, and I have to admit that you aren't far off with respect to my thoughts about helping others become successful in our business. In fact, the little exercise you went through with the Financial /Emotional Matrix really confirmed that the exit option I favor is the right one for me."

"Do tell me more."

"When we plotted me on your diagram before, we agreed that I was just peeking into the upper-right quadrant — reasonably okay financially, but not entirely ready, and somewhat open to retiring, but not fully committed. As I see it, then, my best option is actually a combination of three, which are a) to maximize the value of my business; b) to follow a set plan; and c) to coach or mentor someone to take over my business."

"And we have already started down that path," I suggested. "We've talked about how we can maximize the value of your business and we are developing a plan for your succession. It is only the last step that we have not really discussed. Want to tell me more about your thinking?"

"Sure. It has taken me a while to accept that the best thing for my business and my clients is to bring my successor into the practice sooner rather than later. Given my 'earliest possible' date, theoretically, someone else could be running my business in five years. As you have pointed out, that's not a lot of time to find the right person, strike a deal with them, and integrate them into the business so that clients and staff don't have any concerns and it will be business as usual when I start to make the transition from full-time involvement to something less than that."

"And have you decided what 'something less than that' means?" I asked.

"Not fully — but I know what it *doesn't* mean. It does not mean taking the top clients and working only with them while leaving the rest of the business to my successor to manage. I do not think that is fair to anyone.

"So it is more likely to be continued involvement with the entire business but on a gradually reducing basis, say, over a three- to five-year period. Something like spending a day a week less in the first year, two days a week less in the second year, three days a week less in the third year, and so on. I haven't really worked out the specific details and how ownership and responsibilities would shift from me to my successor over that time, but that would be the general plan. Does it make sense?"

"Absolutely, it does! Again, you have been very thoughtful about what is good for you as well as what's good for the business. Many advisors don't have that duality in mind."

"'Duality' — that's not a word I am that familiar with. Are you trying to impress me?" Henry joked.

"No, not at all," I laughed, "and I apologize if it sounds 'professorial' as you once described me. But it really is a great word to define a situation that has two parts to it that are both complementary and opposed to each other."

"I still don't get it," Henry insisted, although I sensed he was just trying to make sure I knew what I was talking about.

"Let me see if I can explain it another way. If I use the terms 'succession plan' and 'exit strategy,' do you think they mean the same thing or something different?"

"Same thing."

"And most people would agree with you, which is why those two terms are often used interchangeably. I would argue, however, that while they are based on the same event, they represent two different perspectives."

"Which are?"

"I define a succession plan as *what* happens to the *business after the founding advisor is gone*, whereas an exit strategy is *what happens to the founding advisor after the business is gone.*

"I am not trying to be cute, and this is not simply a matter of semantics. It is a very real dilemma faced by every entrepreneur exiting from his or her business. How do I leave the business in the best shape possible while, at the same time, ensuring I get what I want, need, and deserve from the transition? Obviously, we want both the business and the founder to be financially stable and prepared to meet the future after the transition. In that sense, they have complementary objectives.

"However, they can also have opposing objectives because what is good for one may not be good for the other. For example, think about the use of cash in the business. If the founder insists on getting his money out of the business as soon as possible, it may strip all the cash from the firm's bank account or require that a very large percentage of future revenue is paid to him. Either way, it places a huge burden on the business and the successor and may limit their ability to invest in the business, open new markets, etc., all of which may be required for the ongoing viability of the business.

"From the other perspective, if the business pays out the founder 'as little as possible' over an extended period of time, he or she may not be able to enjoy the retirement lifestyle they desire.

"Does that help explain the notion of duality?"

"Yeah, it does. I didn't attach a word to it, but I realized as I was thinking about my transition that I have to look at every decision from two vantage points — as Henry, the owner of my business, and also as Henry, the steward of the rest of my life. I think what I have in mind is good for both."

"I agree! So let me quickly summarize what I think I have heard you say.

"Your intention is to exit your business sometime in the next five to ten years, depending on how your financial freedom and emotional enthusiasm are progressing. Your current belief is that the actual date will be towards the longer end of that term."

"Correct."

"Your plan is to identify a qualified successor soon and, after bringing him or her on board, to gradually reduce the time you spend in the business over a three- to five-year period. You are not going to carve the top clients out for your exclusive work, but rather, you will have your hands in most of the major aspects of operating your business to assist your successor. You will create a transition plan that details roles, responsibilities, compensation, timelines, and so on to ensure everyone's expectations are clear and objectives are aligned.

"In drafting the terms and conditions of the deal with your successor, you will respectfully consider the ongoing needs of the firm as well as your personal lifestyle and other requirements to find the right balance.

"Does that pretty much sum things up so far?"

"Well, I didn't use all the same words, and I think you filled in a few details for me, but essentially, that's the plan. What do you think?"

"Excellent, Henry! Thoughtful, fair, and definitely doable. I hope it also excites and energizes you!"

"It does. There is obviously more to be decided, but as you projected when we first started this exercise, I am starting to control my transition plan. It feels good!"

"That's great, Henry. I am so pleased for you and want to congratulate you on the way in which you have approached our work. Yes, there is more to be done, but you have come such a long way from not wanting to even think about retirement to looking forward to the journey between now and then.

"I think that deserves a nice lunch on me. We can talk about a few more things as we eat, but let's make it a mini-celebration. Are you up for that?"

"If you're buying, I'm not crying," Henry replied. "I know just the expensive place to go!"

Another Illustrative Case in Point

When You Have to Get Out

Rajendra was extremely well known in his community as a politician, leader, and successful businessperson. His past service as a city councillor and Chair of the Budget Committee had exposed him to a large number of prominent citizens, business owners, and government officials. His social skills and business acumen had enabled 'Raj' to leverage those relationships into a profitable financial advisory practice when his term in office expired.

Recently, Raj received word that his father, who lived in India, had been diagnosed with an incurable disease that would slowly take his life over the next three to five years. He would not be in pain through that period; however, his physical capabilities would gradually diminish to the point where he could no longer look after himself. Raj was the eldest child in his family and, as such, was expected to return to India to assist with his father's care and to become head of the family household. That also meant assuming the role of President of his father's export business.

Raj accepted his family responsibility without hesitation. While it meant giving up his flourishing business in North America, there was no doubt he would take on his new role with the same dedication, passion, and energy that had enabled him to build a great practice in his adopted country.

Raj realized he had to make a number of decisions quickly:

- How much time to allow before he relocated to India
- Who to choose to take over his advisory business
- How to maximize the value prior to selling

Fortunately, Raj had always been a forward-looking person, and he had already given thought to his succession plan, even though he had not expected to activate it for at least another ten years.

His first action was a trip to India to gain a better understanding of the situation and to consult with his father. They agreed that Raj could confidently take up to 18 months to make the transition unless, of course, his father's health deteriorated faster than the doctors predicted it would. In his own mind, Raj set a target of 12 months to be on the safe side.

Knowing that he would have no difficulty attracting other advisors interested in acquiring his practice, Raj developed a list of criteria for his successor and identified three associates in his dealer firm whom he thought might qualify. All three were happy to be 'on the short list' and keen to enter into further discussions with Raj.

In Raj's mind, this accomplished two objectives:

- Gave him choice among several good candidates
- Was likely to set up competitive bidding, which would raise the price

Raj indicated he would not enter into an exclusivity or lock-up agreement with any of the candidates but, rather, that he would conduct due diligence on all three simultaneously. Those who successfully met his requirements would be invited to submit a bid for the practice; however, they also had to include a business plan that detailed such areas as:

- Transition plan
- Long-term strategy
- Marketing plan
- Service delivery
- Staffing

Raj also made it clear that the highest bidder would not automatically get the deal.

By the end of the due-diligence process, two of the candidates clearly stood out, so they were invited to submit bids and their business plans. Coincidentally, the advisor who submitted the higher offer also had the most convincing business plan. He was not only willing to pay more for the business, he was going to invest more to assure the long-term success of the transition.

Raj accepted that offer, and they began a 12-month plan to integrate Raj's business with that of the other advisor. Within 18 months, he had relocated to India and started the next stage of his life.

Coach's Recap

- The Financial/Emotional Matrix can be used to identify viable exit options.

- Advisors in the bottom-left corner have neither the financial freedom nor the emotional enthusiasm to retire. Their best option is dig in and work to maximize the value of their business along with their personal assets.
  - As their overall financial capability expands, their emotional enthusiasm will also improve. The short-term objective is to move up or to the right. The longer-term goal is to advance both dimensions sufficiently to provide the freedom of choice.

- Advisors in the upper-left quadrant have a strong emotional desire to exit the business, but limited financial capability.
  - They, too, should work to maximize the value of their business in order to provide more financial freedom to choose when they exit the business.
  - If the emotional desire to exit is very strong, they may want to consider selling to the highest bidder.

- Advisors in the bottom-right quadrant are well positioned financially, but not prepared emotionally.
  - They should work on a plan with a stated timeframe during which they could become more psychologically accepting of the notion of retiring.
  - To gain confidence in their successor, they may want to look for someone they can coach or mentor.

- Advisors in the top-right quadrant have the luxury of choice.
  - They can do whatever they feel is required to leave their business in the best shape possible.

- While it should be everyone's objective to move into the upper-right quadrant, the reality is that not every advisor is going to be that patient and many will never get there.

- Seeking progress is easier than achieving perfection, so the objective should be to move towards what you want.

- While they are based on the same event, *succession plan* and *exit strategy* represent two different perspectives:
  - A succession plan is *what happens to the business after the founding advisor is gone.*
  - An exit strategy is *what happens to the founding advisor after the business is gone.*

My Succession Plan

Exercise #7 – Choosing My Exit Option

1. **My priority interest is:**
   - ☐ What happens to the *business* after I am gone
   - ☐ What happens to *me* after the business is gone
   - ☐ Finding the right balance

2. **Bearing in mind, your previous indication of the quadrant in which your *financial freedom* and *emotional enthusiasm* to transition from your business fell, circle the exit option that is most appropriate for you.**

Financial/Emotional Matrix

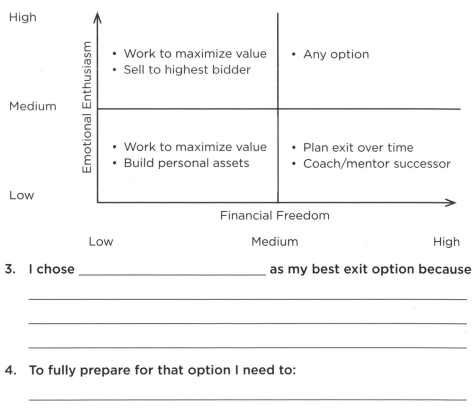

3. I chose _____ as my best exit option because

   _____

   _____

   _____

4. **To fully prepare for that option I need to:**

   _____

   _____

   _____

Definition: KILL v.t. — To leave a vacancy without nominating a successor
The Devil's Dictionary

Chapter 8

Who should be my successor?

As it turned out, Henry and I did not talk about his plan very much over lunch. We actually celebrated his progress with a nice glass of wine, a thoroughly enjoyable meal, and a quiet moment or two of reflection.

Then our conversation turned to the approaching winter and Henry's visit to his brother in Phoenix. One thing he did say was that he was going to talk to his brother about the importance of having something in his retirement lifestyle that gave him joy. He planned to tell him about his own journey of exploration and how it had helped define his retirement plan and give him focus. I reassured him it wasn't too late for his brother to get excited about the next 25 or 30 years of his life — if he could find a cause in which he truly believed to dedicate his time and energy.

By the time we returned to Henry's office, the soothing effects of the wine and food were starting to recede, so we jumped right back into our more structured conversation.

"You know, Henry, the biggest surprise in what you've told me today is your commitment to bringing in a successor early on in the game. I remember you once telling me the last thing you would do is bring some young, perky, wet-behind the-ears, know-it-all advisor into your practice so they can take up all your time, learn everything you know, and then steal your clients away!"

"Yeah, you're right — I did say something like that in a weaker moment. However, that is an example of how I have had to consider what was good for my practice versus what I wanted personally. The best thing for my clients is to have someone whom they already know and trust and is familiar with the way we do business and who will be ready to take over when I start my transition.

"Many of my clients are going to be retired right alongside me, and they shouldn't have to worry about who will provide them with the ongoing advice they need or how they will be treated. I intend to leave my own portfolio and personal insurance program in the hands of my successor. I want my clients to know that I have hand-picked the right person to look after me as well as them."

"It is interesting to hear you express it that way," I said. "Choosing the right successor is, obviously, a critical step in any transition plan, and one of the first questions I ask an advisor when they are considering someone is, 'Would you be willing to have this person manage your financial affairs?' You are already ahead of the game by making that one of the criteria for selection."

"I have always told my clients that I wouldn't recommend anything to them unless I was willing to do it myself, and I won't violate that trust now."

"So, have you thought about what you want to look for in your successor?"

"Well, honesty and integrity are givens. A friendly personality would help. And of course, I'd want them to be smart — about the business and about how they treat my clients and staff."

"How about specific qualifications? Would you expect them to have the same technical knowledge that you do? What about professional credentials, licenses, registrations, etc.?"

"Of course, they'd need to have whatever 'papers' are required to operate, but on the technical knowledge side, I'm not so sure. If they had all the experience and knew everything that I know, they would probably be as old as I am. That would not work!

"Frankly, I'd rather have someone who was willing and capable of learning from me than someone who felt they already knew it all. Someone I could mentor and coach to some extent, as we've said."

"That's music to my ears, Henry. You know how I feel about getting more veteran advisors to take someone less experienced under their wing. And if you have at least five years to work with a younger advisor, as per your plan, you will have lots of time to help them develop the knowledge and skills they'll need to carry on after you transition away from the business."

"We've said this before, but it's worth repeating that this person is going to be the custodian of your legacy, so you want them to reflect your values and respect for others."

"Damn right — or they won't be there!" Henry added emphatically.

"O-kay…," I said somewhat cautiously, given Henry's outburst. "Let's move on to other considerations by first agreeing that there are basically two types of buyers out there — financial and strategic. Financial buyers are interested in one thing — return on their investment. Consequently, they are looking to pay the lowest price possible for a practice or book of business to give them the best upside opportunity.

"Strategic buyers, on the other hand, seek synergy. They are looking for the opportunity to take what they have built and combine it with what you have built to create something greater than the sum of the parts. Of course, strategic buyers don't want to pay any more than they have to, but their motivation is growth rather than ROI. A fair price is more important to them than a low price.

"Because I know you so well, I think we can shorten this discussion and say that you would only be interested in a deal with a strategic buyer."

"Correct!" Henry answered immediately.

"Okay, given that, are you in a position to decide whether your successor will be 'internal' or 'external'? Recall those were two of the exit options we discussed — sale to an 'insider' or sale to someone outside your firm."

"I'd definitely prefer an internal transfer because it is easier to implement and less of a burden on my clients. That being said, no one within my firm immediately comes to mind as the ideal candidate."

"In my experience, few advisors are able to find the 'perfect' successor," I said, "any more than they are able to build their practice exclusively out of 'perfect' clients. So let's look at the pros and cons of each approach. That might help you decide whether you should look more diligently within or accept that you may have to go outside to find the best-qualified candidate. Okay?"

"Go for it!" Henry reacted.

"Since your preference is for an internal transition, let's start there. We previously identified internal candidates as associates working within your current practice or, at least, within your dealer firm. That would also include family members, although, as we also said, there are special considerations for family members that we will need to talk more about if that is something you are considering.

"The big advantage is the relative ease with which the transfer can be made, as you mentioned. I think another huge 'pro' comes from knowing what I refer to as the 'three Ps' — personality, philosophy, and processes. If you have had the chance to work alongside or observe a candidate on the job, you will have a good sense of whether their personality will fit with your clients and staff. You will likely also have some insight into their philosophies with respect to planning, product recommendations, and client service. Finally, if they work in the same firm, they will be accustomed to the company's processes, policies, and procedures. No need for training there.

"If they are already working in your practice, they are likely to have established relationships with at least some of the clients. Even if they are outside your practice, but within the firm, they will have existing relationships with some of the same people you do, such as Head Office staff and product representatives.

"Those people can also give insight into their experience in working with a particular candidate, which can be extremely valuable information, particularly around something like compliance.

"Finally, as we mentioned before, your sponsoring firm may have a program in place to assist with internal transfers. That could run all the way from practice valuation and helping with selection of a successor to financing the transaction and providing administrative support through the transfer of clients.

"Does your firm have such a program in place?"

"Not so much," Henry replied. "They have a video module on our practice management portal and a small booklet that provides general details of the process, but to my knowledge, nothing that comes anywhere near the process we have gone through. In fact, I looked at what they did have available a couple of weeks ago when I was organizing my thoughts. What I found was that, while the firm offered assistance with valuing practices, according to those 'rules of thumb' you dislike so much, they went on to suggest that it might prove valuable to engage an outside consultant with expertise in succession planning or to simply reach out to friends and colleagues who've already gone down this road. Maybe you should talk to them about developing a more robust internal program!"

"I'll certainly do that, Henry, once I am confident I can use you as a role model!" I teased him.

"Humph" was Henry's characteristic reply.

"But, first, let's finish with the pros and cons of considering an internal versus external successor. We have covered the positives of looking inside — now let's consider the challenges. You have already mentioned the most common one — lack of a good candidate. In fact, in an ideal world, you would like to have two or three qualified people among whom you could choose, but that is seldom the case unless you work for a very large firm or in an office with many advisors."

"Yeah, I've done a quick look-through, and I have to say, most of my colleagues are very different from me, and I'm not sure we'd be compatible."

"How are they different, Henry?"

"Personality, work ethic, social skills, even the way some of them dress for the office — just not up to my standards."

"You know, Henry, choosing the right successor doesn't always mean choosing someone like you. Sometimes a change in style or personality can be good, for example, to bring renewed energy and a new perspective into a business. What you really want is someone who can take your practice forward. So if I were you, I'd ask myself such questions as:

- What image do I want my business to have when I am no longer there?

- How do I want my business to grow after I am gone?

- What do the other stakeholders, such as my clients, staff, and family want or need from my successor?

- What competencies do we require in a new leader?

- Can my successor and I work together through the transition?

"If you approached your selection process with these sorts of questions in mind, would any of your colleagues stand up better?"

Henry was quiet for a moment until he finally said, "Yeah, a couple probably would. I'll have to give it more thought."

"Good, but to be sure you're considering everything, let's add a couple more items to the mix that we'd have to count on the 'negative' side of selecting an internal candidate. They include the big one that you expressed a high degree of concern about before — the risk of your intended successor leaving your practice at some point and taking a whack of your clients with them."

Henry jumped right in. "Yeah, I've thought some more about that too, and here's what I have concluded. I have built up very strong relationships with most of my clients — certainly with the top ones. As I mentioned before, many have become friends as well as clients. Unless I have totally misjudged their loyalty to me, I am highly confident that few, if any, would leave me unless I did something totally unethical and personally betrayed their trust. If that ever did occur — which it will not — I would deserve to lose those clients.

"I also think I am a pretty good judge of character, and the likelihood of me choosing a successor who would treat me unfairly after I had given them the chance to take over a great business is slim.

"So if I have clients who choose to leave me to follow someone who takes advantage of me, they are probably not the type of clients I want anyway!"

"I think the risk of that is very low, Henry," I suggested. "And besides, it can be addressed in the actual written transition agreement you'll have with your successor.

"Another thing that could happen is jealousy among your associates. You are going to offer someone a great opportunity in being your successor. Even though you may decide there is only one of your associates who might possibly qualify, others may feel they are at least as deserving, if not more so. I have seen this happen a few times, and it can lead to everything from tensions in the office to outright sabotage of the chosen candidate. I know at least one instance where it was the primary reason an advisor did not want to put a formal succession plan in place. He was an amiable type who did not want to offend anybody."

"That one hadn't occurred to me," Henry said. "I will have to think about that too. Anything else?"

"I think those are the big ones for now. As you get closer to your final decision, others may pop up, but should we move on now to the pros and cons of an external sale?"

"Sure."

"The first advantage of looking outside your firm is, as you have already expressed, a much wider field of potential candidates. Theoretically, you would then be free to choose among all of the advisors in your community and perhaps beyond.

"Secondly, assuming your search leads to a number of qualified prospects, you can almost certainly count on getting multiple competitive offers, which will drive up the price."

"Anything else?" Henry asked.

"Barring having a real 'mad on' with your firm that makes you want to leave them, which I know is not the case with you, another reason I have seen for wanting an external sale is that the advisor genuinely feels his or her clients would be better off somewhere else. That may be due to the current firm not having all the products and services clients may need going forward or a history of seriously bad service."

"I don't think that applies to me," Henry volunteered.

"I don't believe that to be the case either," I agreed. "I just wanted to bring it forward for your information when counselling your own clients. Think about your brother, for example. He sold his plumbing supply business internally, to a couple of employees. He probably could have gotten more money selling to a competitor, but for whatever reason, he chose not to. I am sure much of it had to do with rewarding long-term employees; however, he probably also felt that his clients would be well-served."

"He's the kind of guy who would try to meet both of those objectives," Henry observed.

"I've got a feeling that kind of thinking runs in the family," I responded. Henry just smiled.

"So let's jump now to the negative aspects of an external transfer. I am assuming, first of all, that your contract permits you to transition your business to someone of your choosing?"

"It does."

"Okay, then, over and above the other concern we have already mentioned of it being the one that inconveniences clients the most, there are a few other things to consider.

"One is the time required to sort through a larger number of potential candidates and perform due diligence on those whom you put on your 'short list.' You will want to look more carefully at someone with whom you are not as familiar as you would likely be with an internal colleague. That would include conducting compliance, regulatory, and legal reviews as well as confirming their financial capacity to purchase your business.

"Timing of your investigation and their disclosure will also be a factor. You will only want to let people in to do their due diligence on *your* practice if you think there is a good chance they will be a serious contender. Similarly, most candidates will not be willing to allow you to dig too deeply into their business unless they feel they have a realistic shot at being your successor."

"I can appreciate that," Henry responded.

"Finally, on the negative side of the internal versus external debate, I'd add that external transfers may bring on a higher risk of client defections. That is partly due to the inconvenience factor we already mentioned. However, in my experience, some clients will also use the introduction of a new advisor as an excuse to transfer their accounts to a family member or best friend who is now in the business or to the competitor who has been wooing them for years.

"While they may have stayed with their original advisor through a sense of loyalty or fear there might be some sort of confrontation if they leave, once a new, unfamiliar advisor is in place, they may feel less pressure to continue that relationship. Clearly, that risk is reduced if the new advisor is someone from the same firm or practice and there is an extended period of transition."

"Interesting that you bring that up," Henry interjected. "Just last week I got a call from one of my long-time clients telling me they wanted to transfer their accounts to their son, who had just entered the business, 'to help him get started.' I tried to caution them about the high dropout rate among advisors in the early years without being too negative about their son's likelihood of success, but they were insistent. Hopefully, they don't get locked into something they can't get out of to come back if things don't work out."

"And you aren't even making any immediate changes in your business," I added. "How many more calls like that do you think you'd get if you suddenly announced you were selling your practice to a competitor?"

"A few, to be sure," Henry conceded.

"So, there are pluses and minuses to both internal and external transfers that should be considered as you make your choice. There are also some potential issues that apply to both options."

"Such as?"

"I'd say the big one is the 'chemistry' between you and your successor and the respect you have for each other. If the relationship is built on a strong foundation, you have a far better chance of managing any conflicts that pop up through the transition period, particularly if that period is a lengthy one."

"What sorts of conflicts?" Henry asked.

"Misunderstanding or misinterpretation of the 'deal,'" I suggested, "can lead to misaligned expectations that can cause what starts off as a good transition experience to deteriorate over time.

"There is also the issue of the value of each individual's contribution. Like any other partnership, if one person believes they are doing most of the work but still have shared all the rewards, they may feel mistreated. I have heard buyers and sellers argue over what the founder's 'sweat equity' is worth compared to the financial contribution the successor is making.

"What if it turns out after a while that one party simply decides the whole structure of the succession plan no longer works for them or there isn't a good 'fit' or they simply change their mind?"

"How often do those things happen?" Henry asked with a bit of apprehension in his voice.

"The bad news is, more often than they should," I answered, "but the good news is, much less often than they used to. Both buyers and sellers have become more sophisticated in their approach to a transaction over the past few years and now address most of these contingencies in their formal agreement. Getting a 'divorce' after the fact can be both legally complicated and very expensive.

"Which brings me to another important consideration, regardless of where your successor comes from — and that is their ability to pay. Because you will be looking for the sale of your practice to fund part of your retirement lifestyle, you will want reassurance that your successor has the financial capability to either pay you full price upfront, which seldom happens, or to make a sufficiently large down payment and meet any ongoing earn-out obligations.

"Given that they will represent your legacy, you will also likely want some confidence they can weather negative markets, expand the business, retain the staff, and service the clients."

"Again, lots of decisions to be made," Henry observed, somewhat distractedly.

"Yes, there are, but don't be discouraged. Once you have those 'big rock decisions' around timing and exit option in place, a lot of choices eliminate themselves. I'm giving you the 'full meal deal,' so to speak, so you can apply it to your work with your clients and their succession plans, but you are already well along the path.

"Recall from our previous work together how important I insisted it was to have a well-defined vision for your business? Having that mental picture of what you wanted your world to look like down the road, made the rest of your decisions easier. If something took you towards that vision, you pursued it. If it took you away from it, you ignored it.

"Same thing here — when you can articulate what you want your succession to look and feel like, the rest falls into place. Your plan may not be simple to implement, but it will be easier to stay on target. You are getting close!"

Another Illustrative Case in Point

People Change Their Minds

Lisa had built a great practice, and when she turned 55, she created a succession plan — a full ten years before her targeted retirement date. She knew she wanted an internal transition to someone she had trained and coached.

Lisa considered a number of candidates from within her own firm but could not identify anyone she felt had the right attitude and aptitude to be her eventual successor. So she initiated a search outside the industry for someone she could mold and train. Given that she had ten years before her plan went into effect, she felt she had lots of time to prepare someone for the role.

Eventually, Lisa met a bright, engaging young woman, Sally, who seemed to have the requisite attributes. After a number of meetings and various testing processes, Lisa offered Sally the position of executive assistant with the intention that she would become an advisor and someday take over the business. Sally enthusiastically accepted.

In fact, Sally turned out to be an incredibly talented and loyal associate who demonstrated every characteristic Lisa wanted in her successor. Clients and staff adored her, she was smart about the business, and she loved taking on more and more responsibility.

As the years passed, Sally qualified as an advisor, completed her CFP designation, and began to take on more and more client relationships. She also took a greater role in the management of the business. Eventually, Sally had to hire her own executive assistant so she could focus more on business development and client relationships. This allowed Lisa to begin to spend less time in the business as she prepared for her retirement.

It seemed like the perfect plan, and everything was progressing very nicely towards a planned transition in about a year's time, when Sally's husband received an out-of-the-blue and out-of-this-world offer to head up his company's operations in Europe. It came with a huge employment contract and all the 'perks' of a very senior executive.

It was a gut-wrenching decision for Sally and her husband to make the choice between his career in Europe and hers here. The deciding factor turned out to be their children's "education in life," as Sally described it. She and her husband concluded that their children might never again have the opportunity to experience different cultures, learn a new language or two, and "see the world," so with great regret, Sally walked away from her potential ownership of the business she and Lisa had been working on together for almost ten years.

Sally's decision obviously knocked the wind right out of Lisa and her plan. While she did not feel the years working with Sally had been wasted, she felt pretty much right back where she started ten years prior.

Fortunately, Lisa had learned a great deal through her mentoring of Sally, so she was able to short-circuit finding and integrating another successor — but it did set her own retirement plans back a couple of years.

More important, Lisa never really got over the feeling that her succession plan had 'failed' and that her retirement did not bring with it the satisfaction she had expected.

Coach's Recap

- Choosing the right successor is a critical step in any transition plan.

- Choosing the right successor does not always mean choosing someone like you. Sometimes a change in style or personality can bring renewed energy and a new perspective into a business.

- One of the questions to ask yourself is "Would I be willing to have this person manage my financial affairs?"

- There are two types of buyers — financial and strategic.

- Financial buyers are interested in return on their investment.
    - They look to pay the lowest price possible to give them the best upside

- Strategic buyers seek synergy
    - They look to combine what they have built with what you have built to create something greater than the sum of the parts
    - Strategic buyers' motivation is growth rather than ROI
    - A fair price is more important to them than a low price

- Transfers can be "internal" or "external."

- The advantages of internal transitions include:
    - Ease with which the transfer can be made
    - Better knowledge of candidate's personality and philosophies
    - Less need for training in company policies and processes
    - May already have relationships with existing clients
    - May be able to use current firm's succession assistance programs

- The disadvantages of internal transitions include:
    - Risk of your successor leaving your practice and taking clients with them
    - Jealousy among your associates who did not get the opportunity to become your successor

- The advantages of external transitions include:
    - A much wider field of potential candidates
    - Likely to receive multiple competitive offers, driving price up
    - Opportunity to offer clients products and services not currently available

- The disadvantages of external transitions include:
    - Time required to sort through a larger number of potential candidates and perform due diligence on your "short list"
    - Opening up your practice to due diligence by potential purchaser
    - Higher risk of client defections

- Other potential issues:
    - "Chemistry" between you and your successor
    - Misunderstanding or misinterpretation of the "deal"
    - Valuation of each individual's contribution
    - One party decides the plan no longer works or isn't a good "fit"
    - Assurance your successor has the financial capability to pay you, as well as weather markets, expand the business, retain staff, and service clients

My Succession Plan

Exercise #8 – Who Should Be My Successor?

1. **My preference for transitioning my practice would be:**
    - ☐ Internal sale to someone within my firm
    - ☐ External sale to a competitor or non-related buyer
    - ☐ Transition to a family member
    - ☐ Other (Specify) _____

2. **My successor should meet the following criteria:** (Provide details)
    - ☐ Age _____
    - ☐ Years in business _____
    - ☐ Licensing _____
    - ☐ Education _____
    - ☐ Designations _____
    - ☐ Experience with similar clients _____
    - ☐ Personal values _____
    - ☐ Attitude _____
    - ☐ Philosophies _____
    - ☐ Personality _____
    - ☐ Financial strength _____
    - ☐ Other (Specify) _____
    - ☐ Other (Specify) _____

3. **Are there any "knock-out" factors or non-negotiable items that would prevent you from transitioning your practice to an individual?** _____

    _____

    _____

4. **Is there anyone to whom you would definitely NOT want to transition your business? If so, why?** _____

    _____

    _____

5. **I have a candidate in mind.**
    - ☐ Yes (Name) _____   ☐ No

"Live, love, laugh… leave a legacy."
Stephen Covey

Chapter 9

What about family as successor?

"Now, it has been a long but, I think, very productive day, Henry. I suggest we wrap it up for now to give you some breathing room to consider what we have talked about.

"Before we do so, however, is there anything else weighing heavily on your mind right now?"

"Well, actually, there is one more question I'd like to explore, but we can leave it for another day."

"Tell me what it is first, and then we can decide when to pursue it."

"We have alluded to this a couple of times, and I am not convinced it is even all that practical or realistic. I can see pros and cons, and I'm pretty sure you won't agree with it, but it is something I have been thinking about…"

"For Heaven's sake, Henry, what is it?" I interrupted.

"Okay," he said, mustering up his courage. "What about me bringing my son into the practice as my successor? I think it would be great if he could carry on 'the family business,' so to speak."

I paused for a moment before answering, partly to allow Henry's anxiety around the question to calm down, but also to organize my own thoughts.

Finally, I said, "That's every entrepreneur's dream, Henry — to be able to pass all the benefit of their years of building their business along to a child, or children if that is the case — so I am not at all surprised that you are considering it.

"Since our discussions today have been all about choosing the right successor, I think we should take a few more minutes now to at least begin to explore the option of your son being that person. I assume you are up for that."

"Definitely!" Henry declared with such intensity that I knew it had been on his mind all day and explained his obvious distraction during our conversation.

"First, let me emphasize that everything we talked about in terms of qualifications for your successor applies equally, if not more so, when it comes to family members. If there is any relief from that, it is that family members are 'insiders,' which means they enjoy the benefits of being an 'internal' option. In general, as we discussed, clients prefer internal transitions, and I would go even further and say that, *all other things being equal*, they would rather see a family member take over a business than a stranger.

"The operative phrase here, however, is *all other things being equal*. As I have indicated in earlier conversations, there are special considerations when passing the torch to family."

"And they would be?" Henry asked with a more serious tone to his voice.

"First, tell me — as far as I know, your son is not in the business today — correct?"

"No, he is not. But he is a smart guy and a fast learner."

"I'm not questioning that at all. Have you ever talked to him about joining you?"

"When he was in high school, he worked part time in the office and full time during the summer, helping out with the administrative work when some of the staff was on vacation. I said to him at that time, that perhaps he ought to consider a career as an advisor, but the discussion never went very far. When he graduated from college, however, he got swept away by the allure of a job in a high-profile software company. That company isn't doing so well today, and I know he is concerned about his future. The timing might be perfect for him to consider a career change."

"Perhaps so, and if this something you want to seriously consider, I do think you should ask him about it sooner rather than later so that you are both aware of how each other feels about the possibility. Before you do that, however, I would suggest you try to answer a few questions on your own."

"Such as?"

"For example, you have a very powerful belief in the value of the work you do for your clients. Do you think your son shares that passion or, at least, could develop it? It's part of what's driven you to be so successful."

"He has a sincere interest in helping others, much as I do. He has always been involved in some community activity that enables him to do some good for somebody," Henry answered.

"That's certainly commendable," I offered," but there is a big difference between contributing at the level you are describing and making it your life's work. Do you think he would be up for that kind of commitment?"

"I'd hope so," Henry replied, "but I'm not sure."

I continued, "Do you know what his real passion in life is? Is there a chance he has something else he desperately wants to do?

"Let me give you an example of what I mean. I was recently involved in a coaching engagement for a well-established husband and wife practice, where they naturally assumed their son would come into the business since they had been contemplating it for years. They asked me to have dinner with them and their son to 'talk up' all the good things about being an advisor and how lucky he was to have the opportunity to carry on in his parents' footsteps.

"Our conversation started down that path, but it was soon obvious to me the son's heart wasn't really into our discussions. So I stopped right in the middle of our meal and asked him point blank if he really wanted to be an advisor in the family practice and eventually own it. After a couple of anxious looks at his parents, he finally said, 'No, I want to be an airline pilot.'

"His parents were obviously shocked, and after a few protests from them, our dinner table fell quiet for what seemed like an eternity until the son finally said, 'I'm sorry Mom and Dad, I know that's what you want for me, but it's not what I want for myself.'

"'Why didn't you say something before?' his mother asked. 'We've talked about this so many times.' To which he replied, 'Because I didn't want to disappoint you.'"

I let that sink in with Henry for a moment before continuing. "Too many businesses have failed in the transition from one generation to the next because a parent assumed the child wanted to be 'just like Dad or Mom' when what the child felt was an obligation to the family that they didn't want to bear. When businesses pass from parents to children under those conditions, they almost inevitably start to deteriorate right away and eventually fail completely."

"You're right. I do not really know what his passions in life are today and how he would like his future to unfold. I can see the importance of that conversation," Henry conceded.

"Let me add a couple more questions for you to think about, as well as include in the conversation with your son, beginning with work ethic."

"Oh, he has always been a hard worker," Henry jumped in, "whether it was at school, in sports, whatever."

"I don't doubt that he inherited your values around hard work," I said, "but what I am talking about is extraordinary effort — the kind that would show everyone around him — clients, staff, other associates — that he deserves to be your successor, not because he is 'Daddy's boy.' I know that sounds a bit harsh, but again, in the real world, there are going to be people around him who, if they aren't expecting or hoping he will fail, won't be cheering for him."

"Like those other advisors we talked about who think they should be my successor," Henry added.

"Yes, like those people and, curiously, a few who actually like *you* so much, no one else could possibly ever measure up in their minds. Or, perhaps, they fear change of any kind, and while their feelings may not be overtly obvious, their conscious or unconscious lack of support could make things tough for any successor."

"I don't think I have anyone like that around me," Henry challenged.

"It's great that you feel that way, Henry, and I hope you are right. The possibility, however, is something to be aware of and to discuss with your son.

"In a similar way, are there other children in your family who think they, perhaps, should have the same opportunity to take over the family business someday?

"If so, how will you and your son deal with that? I recently witnessed a situation where there were two adult children in a family where the father was retiring.

One child very much wanted to take over Papa's practice. The other did not but insisted on being given a place in the business at a high salary 'in fairness,' as they described it.

"The father relented, and I think you can guess the outcome. One child worked very hard to continue to build the business while the other often showed up late, did not complete their work, and generally was not interested in the success of the practice. In the end, the child who was building the business had to 'buy out' their sibling, which meant paying two other people — the father and the sibling — before paying themselves. Not a great way to start a new career!"

"Fortunately, as you know," Henry said in defense, "my daughter, who is my only other child, is a professional classical musician who has absolutely no interest in what I do. She has enjoyed the benefits, but her passion is music, arts, theatre — things like that. Business is an anathema to her, so that's not a risk for us."

"I suspected not but wanted to mention it because situations like the one I described could come up in your work with your business-owner clients around their succession planning.

"And that example reminds me to talk about the financial challenges that sometimes accompany bringing a family member into the business."

"Why would the financial aspects be different from any other scenario?" Henry asked.

"Well, let me ask you this question, 'Would you expect your son to pay you the same price for your business as anyone else?'"

Henry thought a bit before answering, "Well, I'd probably give him a 'family discount' of some sort."

"How much of a discount?"

"I don't know."

"Would you hold him to the same terms regarding down payment, residual payments, penalties for missed instalments, and so on?"

"I don't know."

"How will he feel about having to pay you as he assumes ownership of the business and while he is working very hard to build his own personal wealth?"

"I don't know."

"Obviously, you are free to make any decisions you want around the financial deal you might offer your son; however, each concession that you give him affects your retirement income situation. As we have talked about before, how do you strike the balance between what is good for you and what is good for your successor — in this case, your son?"

"I don't know."

"So it sounds like a long and very specific conversation with your son is in order if he is to be potentially considered as your successor."

"It certainly does, and I want to have that conversation," Henry said with some determination in his voice.

"Great. I certainly encourage you to do that. In addition, remember that whatever plan you make with anyone — your son, an associate, or a complete stranger — will always have some element of compromise associated with it. Your decision is about what you are willing to give up in order to get what you want.

"If, at the end of the day, *when all things are considered*, your son turns out to be the best candidate — that would be great! Again an operative phrase 'when all things are considered.' If you do not really believe that he is the best choice, pick someone else.

"I keep repeating this, but it's your legacy. From a very practical standpoint, a poor choice can be expensive if clients leave or the business falters and your payout is at risk, along with your reputation. Your successor is a reflection of you, and your clients trust you to leave them in good hands.

"I apologize, Henry, if you think I have been a little hard on you with respect to this part of our conversation today. This is a very serious decision because it not only affects your life, but your son's as well. Have I given you enough to think about?"

"More than enough," Henry answered with just a hint of annoyance in his voice. "I am not giving up on the idea of my son joining me to eventually take over the business, but I better recognize the challenges now. I will get together with him for a candid conversation, and we'll see what comes of it."

"Excellent! I would suggest you do that before we get together again. The outcome of that discussion will certainly give us direction in bringing more definition to your plan.

"I am also going to have a copy of a great book by a friend of mine delivered to your office. His name is Tom Deans and his book *Every Family's Business — 12 Common Sense Questions to Protect Your Wealth* [1] has sold more than half-a-million copies worldwide. It really opens people's minds to the issues around passing the 'family business,' as you called it, to the next generation.

"Will you promise me that you'll read the book before you meet with your son? It is not too long but packs a very powerful message, and I think it will be a big help to you in having that conversation."

"Of course, if you are recommending it, I'll read it," Henry responded.

"Excellent, then may I leave it to you to contact me after you've read Tom's book and had the meeting with your son?"

"Yeah," Henry answered, but I wasn't quite sure he even realized he had said that. He had that familiar faraway look in his eyes that told me his mind was still hard at work trying to find the answers to some important questions.

———

Almost a month passed before I heard from Henry. He told me on the telephone that he had read Tom Deans' book *Every Family's Business* and had the conversation with his son as we discussed. He was ready to talk more about his transition plan, so we scheduled a meeting.

"So, how did the discussion with your son go?" I asked once we got through the pleasantries.

"Better than I expected," Henry responded, "but, perhaps, not quite as well as I hoped."

"How so?"

"On the 'better-than-expected' side, my son and I probably had the best conversation we've had together in several years. In fact, we actually had two conversations, about two weeks apart. I learned things about him that I did not know, and I was reminded of why I think he is such a good kid. He is smart,

---

1   Every Family's Business – Tom Deans, PhD – http://everyfamiliesbusiness.com

thoughtful, and considerate. I have always felt that way, but it was great to be reminded of why. There were times I was just beaming with pride. He isn't just my son anymore — he is a very mature young man with lots of ambition and ideas about what he wants in life."

"I am not at all surprised by that," I offered. "He's had a pretty good role model!"

"Thanks, but I think he is much further ahead in his thinking and determination than I was at his age. Which brings me to the 'not-as-well-as-I'd-hoped' part of our discussions. He does not want to be my successor."

I paused before reacting. "How do you feel about that — disappointed, I am sure?"

"Yeah, of course I am. As you said, it's every entrepreneur's dream that one of his children will follow in his footsteps. But I definitely respect my son's decision and, based on the discussions he and I had, I think it is probably best for me as well."

"Do you want to tell me more about your conversation, or should I say… conversations?"

"Well, I started by reading Tom Deans' book, *Every Family's Business*, as you suggested. His 12 questions were certainly thought-provoking, as I am sure you knew they would be, and they got me looking at my business in a different way."

"How so?" I asked.

"I came to the realization that I was guilty of the same thinking that I have criticized in some of my clients, in that I never really thought of my business as part of my investment portfolio per se. Once I accepted that it was, it became clear that any decisions about whether to 'hold' or 'sell' should be made in the same way I would make them for any other investment. That would mean selling when the price was up, to the most qualified buyer.

"In most cases, the most qualified buyer would be the highest bidder; however, as we have discussed, when it comes to a business as personal as giving people financial advice that will affect them for the rest of their lives, the 'most qualified buyer' isn't necessarily the one willing to pay the highest price. All that said and done, I have to conclude that my son is not the most qualified buyer. If he isn't going to be fully committed to the business, I have to find someone else."

"And you don't feel he would be fully committed?" I had to ask.

"I thought he could be," Henry responded, "but more important than my opinion is the fact that he concluded he wouldn't be. It's not what he wants to do with his life, and he doesn't want to come to me at some point down the road and say he has changed his mind."

"I am curious as to how your two conversations played out. Do you mind sharing the details?"

"Not at all. Armed with some of the questions from Tom Deans' book and my own thoughts, I organized a lunch at the club for us. He knew something was up because it is something we have only done a few times before, so I had to reassure him I wasn't dying or something. I simply said that I had to make some decisions about my business and that I would value his opinion as someone who had witnessed how it had evolved over his lifetime and the impact that it had on our family."

"Good positioning," I congratulated Henry.

"I didn't want to be too direct until we were face to face."

"When we met, I described the work you and I have been doing together — how reluctant I was to discuss my retirement at the beginning, but how I became convinced it wasn't too soon to start making plans for my eventual transition from the business. He asked quite a few questions, as you did, about my emotional readiness to quit the business I had spent so much time building and appeared to love so much. I guess that's what he observed as a child, and I think that is when I realized how grown up he was. His questions were thoughtful and right on the mark."

"Isn't it amazing how much more perceptive our children are than we ever give them credit for?" I said.

"Yes, it is indeed!" Henry reacted.

"What else did you discuss? I assume you are still talking about the first meeting?"

"Yes, I am. From there, I got into more of the specifics of the conversations you and I have had. I told him about my 'earliest possible' and 'latest acceptable' dates. I outlined my plan to bring someone younger into the business and to work with them over an extended period while I gradually reduced my involvement until they were fully integrated into the business and clients were comfortable with them. I also told him about my idea of becoming a coach to my entrepreneur clients through succession from their own businesses."

By this point, I was trying hard not to smile too much as Henry described all of *his ideas*. Nothing pleases a coach as much as having someone take your guidance and turn it into their own wise self-counsel!

Henry continued. "Then I got to the part about the importance of selecting the right successor and making the choice between *internal* and *external* and how I much preferred that person be someone I already knew and respected.

"He agreed with me completely. That is when I decided the time was right to ask him straight up if he was interested. So I simply said that internal successors were often family members and it had occurred to me that he might be the ideal candidate."

"How did he react?" I asked.

"He didn't right away. Obviously, he wasn't expecting the question, so I could sense the wheels were turning in his head as he was putting things in perspective."

"Like father, like son," I thought to myself amusedly.

"Then he finally said that he was flattered and honored. How's that coming from a child to a parent?" Henry boasted proudly.

"He went on to say that I'd caught him by surprise and it wasn't something he had ever given much thought, although he did recall our brief conversations about it when he was a teenager working in the office during the summer. He admitted he had not paid much attention back then and hadn't taken it as a serious possibility.

"At that point, he said he could not, obviously, answer yes or no, but that he would think about it. I said that was all I was asking and that he should not feel any pressure or obligation. I repeated the story you told me about the parents whose son had to tell them, after years of them thinking he would take over the family practice, that he would rather be an airline pilot but was afraid to say so for fear of disappointing them. I said I'd never want my son to be in that position."

"Is that how the first meeting ended?" I asked.

"No, and this is where I was really impressed by him again. He started asking all kinds of questions about the business — how it operated, how clients were developed and serviced, what technology we used, what the staff did versus what

I did, and so on. He went on to ask about the industry — the challenges and opportunities that existed, how firms differentiated themselves, and the changes I foresaw.

"I did my best to answer, but I knew he was going to do his own research anyway. He is that kind of guy. The one big thing we had not discussed to that point was the financial side of things. So I told him about the valuation you had done, and I think he was taken back by the value of my practice. I don't believe he ever suspected it could be worth that much!"

"It could come as a shock to someone outside the business who has little perspective on how value is created in a financial advisory practice. Even though your son personally observed your progress in business, he probably couldn't relate to it."

"I guess not," Henry agreed. "However, that led us into a discussion about how the value of the business was important to me for my own retirement planning and that someday it would be sold. I repeated that my preference would be to sell it to him and joked a bit about a 'family discount.'

"I then gave him my copy of Tom Deans' book and said that it presented a sober view of the challenges of inter-generational transfer of businesses. I asked him to read it and to agree to meet again for further discussion. He promised he would do that, and so we set a date for two weeks hence to get together again."

"Henry, I have to congratulate you — and your son — for the seriousness and thoroughness with which you have approached this topic. I know how sensitive it can be, and I have seen similar situations blow up completely because one or both parties was either offended or felt mistreated in some way. You guys demonstrated the great trust and respect you have for each other."

"As I said, I gained a new perspective on my son, and I am very proud of him!" Henry beamed.

"And so you should be," I agreed, "and as *I* said, he had a great mentor!

"So, how about the second meeting; is that when he said no to your offer?"

"Yes, it is, although I have to say I have seldom been turned down so graciously!" Henry said.

"My son first congratulated me on what I had accomplished with my business.

He said he was not only impressed by the value I had created, but also the professional manner in which the practice was being run. He said he was proud of me! It almost brought tears to my eyes.

"He went on to say that he recognized he was being offered an incredible opportunity and repeated how flattered and honored he was. All that being said, however, he was going to decline."

"Was he specific as to why?"

"Yeah, he said he'd thought about it long and hard but had concluded it just wasn't the career for him. He was not sure he could develop the 'itch,' as he described it, for the work that I did or that he was qualified to be the 'custodian of my legacy.' Funny how he used that term — I don't think I ever mentioned it to him, but obviously, he understood that responsibility.

"He also said that, while his current position in his firm was tenuous, he wanted to stay in the software industry. He had some ideas for a specialized application of his own, and he wanted to follow it through. He had gone so far as to recruit a couple of people to the idea and was already talking to others who were interested in financing his venture.

"When I suggested to him that I could wait a couple of years to see how things worked out for him, he said, 'Dad, that's not your plan. You need to get going on your plan right away — it's important. Besides that, if this project doesn't work out, I'll try another. Most great software entrepreneurs failed a number of times before they succeeded. It's part of the game, and I'm up for it!'

"I pretty much knew then and there that there wasn't anything I could say to change his mind. He had his own passion he wanted to pursue and he was not going to be swayed from trying. All I could really do was support and encourage him — so that is what I have decided to do.

"My son won't be coming into my business, but I am going to do what I can to maximize its value before I sell it so I can be in a position to help him financially if he needs it. At the very least, when I die, I want to leave him some of the family wealth so he can follow his dream."

"Wow, Henry, what beautiful thoughts!" I said. "You are a great father, and I have no doubt your son will make his own mark in the world that will continue to make you proud.

"Thanks for sharing all this with me. In addition to giving you the satisfaction that you and your son came to the same conclusion with respect to his career, another very positive thing it does for us is to eliminate one of your exit options, clearing the way for you to choose another. Are you getting close to making any more decisions about that?"

"Yes, with this matter settled, I think I have it narrowed down. However, can I have a week or so to finalize my thoughts? I am still recovering a bit from my son's decision."

"Of course," I said. "Take some time. I will check in with you in about ten days to see how you are doing. Okay?"

"That would be fine,' was Henry's reply. Once again, I could see the distant look in his eyes as he was trying to absorb everything that had happened and its impact on his future. I knew by our next meeting that he would have a fix on what he wanted to happen.

Another Illustrative Case in Point

When Children Just Don't Cut It

Morris had pretty much done it all in the business. He began as an insurance advisor in a career agency company when he was only 25 years old and then moved to his firm's Home Office to be part of their internal management development program. While there, he worked primarily in the Training Department, creating educational programs, conducting workshops, and doing joint field work with new advisors.

After two years "on the inside," the company posted Morris to a large branch office as an Assistant Manager to one of the firm's most successful Branch Managers. Three years after that, the Branch Manager retired, and Morris took over that role. For the next five years, he continued the branch's success until the Home Office asked him to return to head up the introduction of investment products to a predominantly insurance-based field force.

Morris carried out that mandate until an international mutual fund manager recruited him as their chief business development officer, a position he held until the firm merged with another of similar size to become one of the largest in the industry. There was considerable redundancy within the management ranks of the merged firm, and Morris did not really like the new culture, so he accepted a buyout package and left to begin the next phase of his career.

Missing the "action" of the field, Morris used the money from his buyout to acquire the insurance business of an advisor he knew who was retiring. He added investment products to the practice's offering and expanded the business significantly through acquisition of several small books of business.

Approaching his 55th birthday, Morris began to think about his retirement. Like most entrepreneurs, he knew he would love to pass his business onto one or more of his children. In particular, his daughter, Cynthia, seemed to be the most interested and capable. Despite his experience in the business, Morris did not feel he was the best person to train his daughter. He thought she would probably have the best learning experience by joining the rookie training program at a large national firm. Once she had a couple of years' experience, she could join her father's business with the view of one day leading it. Cynthia thought taking over the "family business" was "cool," so she agreed to the plan.

Morris watched his daughter's progress closely over the next two and a half years. He often had conversations with her about her business and how she could grow it more quickly. While Cynthia was doing all right at the other firm, Morris had seen enough advisors come and go throughout his career to know that something was missing. He eventually concluded that, unless Cynthia became more engaged and productive, she would not have the attributes necessary for a long-term career as an advisor, let alone the owner of a thriving practice.

In a "heart-to-heart" conversation one day, Morris shared his concerns with Cynthia. At first, she protested that he had it all wrong and was expecting too much of her. After a while, however, Cynthia conceded that she occasionally had similar thoughts about her suitability for the industry. While there were parts of the business she enjoyed, there were a few important parts she did not — particularly, prospecting and developing new clients. Her thinking, however, had always been that, once she joined her father, those things would be less important because he already had an established client base.

Morris patiently explained how important those activities would always be in any practice and how they would be a major responsibility of whoever led the firm. He asked Cynthia to take some time to think about her willingness to accept that responsibility and to do those things for the rest of her career.

Within a week, Cynthia informed Morris that, after careful consideration, she no longer wanted to be a candidate to take over his business.

Coach's Recap

- It is every entrepreneur's dream to be able to pass all the benefit of their years of building their business along to a child or children.

- *All other things being equal,* clients would rather see a family member take over a business than a stranger.

- Every qualification for your successor applies equally, if not more so, when it comes to family members.

- In considering family members as potential successors, ask yourself if they:
  - Have the same passion for the industry
  - Value the work in the same way you do
  - Feel an obligation to carry on "the family business"
  - Have the required work ethic
  - Can manage siblings and other wannabe successors
  - Have the financial capacity to pay you and them

- Your business is part of your investment portfolio. Make any decisions about whether to "hold" or "sell" in the same way as any other investment:
  - Sell when value is up
  - Sell to the most qualified buyer
  - The highest bidder may not be the most qualified buyer

- The value of your practice can come as a shock to someone outside the business who has little perspective on how that value is created.

My Succession Plan

Exercise #9 – What About Family as Successor?

1. **I am willing to consider a family member as my successor**

   ☐ No ☐ Yes (Name) _____

2. **If "Yes", it would be important for them to have the following characteristics:** (Check all that apply and describe)
   - ☐ Age _____
   - ☐ Industry experience _____
   - ☐ Technical knowledge _____
   - ☐ Client management experience _____
   - ☐ Reputation _____
   - ☐ "Fire in the belly" _____
   - ☐ Passionate about the business _____
   - ☐ Willing to give "extra effort" _____
   - ☐ No obligation to carry on the business_____
   - ☐ Have/can earn respect of clients and staff _____
   - ☐ Willing and able to invest in the business _____
   - ☐ Able to manage sibling relationships _____
   - ☐ Other (Specify) _____
   - ☐ Other (Specify) _____

3. **If "Yes", my potential family successor:**
   - ☐ Exceeds most qualification
   - ☐ Meets most qualifications
   - ☐ Falls short of some qualifications
   - ☐ Fall short of most qualifications

4. **Overall, I feel _____'s potential as my successor is:**

   ☐ Excellent ☐ Good ☐ Fair ☐ Poor

"Nobody can go back and start a new beginning, but anyone can start today and make a new ending."
Maria Robinson

Chapter 10

How do I set myself up for success?

Two weeks passed before Henry and I got together again, and the first thing I noticed was a bit of bluster in his demeanor and much more confidence in his voice than when we last met. I felt I had to comment.

"Henry, you seem to have a bit of swagger in your step and the slight look of excitement in your eyes."

"I don't know what you're talking about," he reacted, with just enough feigned disinterest for me to know I had hit it right.

"I've been very busy with clients recently — year-end stuff, you know — I guess the intensity is showing."

"Nothing else?" I asked.

"Like what?" he responded somewhat sarcastically.

"Like because you have made some decisions about your transition plan, you are feeling pretty good about it?"

"Humph," he replied with less curtness before confessing, "Well, I guess by now you can read me pretty well. I have come to some more conclusions… and I admit — it does feel good."

"That's fabulous, Henry. I can't wait to hear what you've decided."

"We have pretty much covered the big picture in our previous conversations — I want to transition out of my business sometime in the next five to ten years. That means starting to look now for a qualified younger advisor or, perhaps, even two advisors who can eventually take over my practice completely. I want to have them in place within the next 12 months.

"I'm thinking someone in their late 30s or early 40s with at least ten years' experience in the business. They should be old enough to have demonstrated their capabilities, yet young enough that they will have 15 to 20 years after I am gone to run the business and eventually find their own successor."

"So how do you intend to attract this superstar candidate?" I asked.

"By showing them what a huge opportunity is waiting for them not too far down the road if we work together. Through our combined efforts, we can create a business that is far better than either one of us could separately."

"That sounds good, Henry, but I think the type of person you describe will want more than a pretty picture of the future before they make that commitment. What can you specifically offer them to demonstrate *your* commitment?"

"We'll put a plan in place that specifically details how they can acquire equity — timing, pricing model, terms, etc. I am not going to give the business away. They will have to earn the right to buy it; however, I will be fair and reasonable because I know I am asking them to dedicate their lives for a few years to making the business more valuable — to me and to them.

"Operationally between now and then, I will gradually reduce my day-to-day participation in running the practice, but I will still be involved in any aspect of the business that requires my attention. We will have a development plan with milestones that dictates how, when, and what management responsibilities they will assume. By my 'earliest possible' date — five years from now — I would expect them to be fully capable of running the business, so the transition should be smooth.

"From a compensation standpoint, we will have defined job descriptions and performance measurements. We will compensate everyone according to their role and equity position by following the 'advisor comp' vs 'owner comp' model you and I talked about previously — fair pay for their work as advisors, some amount for their management duties, and a share of the profits according to their percentage of ownership.

"In my advisor role, my plan is to add 'succession planning' to my list of services and capabilities I can provide to clients. I will make that a focus of my conversations and activities with current business-owner clients and centers of influence. In that way, I can leverage my existing relationships to create new revenue development opportunities, which will grow my business more purposely and aggressively than if I simply continue to service my current clients and receive the occasional referral to a prospective new client.

"Finally, I want to be sure I have something to retire to that really excites me. I want to make a contribution to someone or something where I can make a difference. Part of that will come from coaching and mentoring my successor, but I know there will be something else I can do. I don't know yet what that might be specifically, but I have a few years to sort that one out, and I am confident I will."

"Wow, Henry," I said. "That is one of the most considered and best articulated, high-level transition plans I have ever heard! Sure there are lots of details behind each of those statements, but if every advisor I encountered was as thoughtful about their transition plan as you have been, I wouldn't have anyone to coach!"

"I guess I have you to thank," Henry admitted with contrived reluctance. "You led me through a process of self-discovery that allowed me to think deeply about what I want out of the rest of my life."

"Well, I appreciate your gratitude," I said with an equally artificial nonchalance.

"What really excites me about what you have just described is how you nailed a number of the key elements of a great succession — and I bet you don't even realize how clever you've been!"

"Well, do tell!" Henry insisted.

"First off," I began, "even though you didn't use the exact words, you made a distinction between transfer of ownership and transfer of management. In the first case, you talked about having *a plan in place that specifically details how they can acquire equity,* and then you said that you would have *a development plan with milestones that dictates how, when and what management responsibilities they will assume.*

"Not every advisor recognizes that difference when designing their transition plan. Many think of ownership and management as being the same thing because that's how they operate when they are sole practitioners — simultaneously, as both owner and manager. When a successor enters the picture, however, it is important to consider the division of those two activities.

"It's not that they aren't linked together, but they don't have to move in lock-step with each other. You can transfer partial ownership over time, as you intend to do, without giving up all management responsibilities, or vice versa. Separating your compensation plan makes that easier."

"I can see now how having a detailed plan in place for the transition is important, even among the best of friends," Henry observed.

"Absolutely!" I said. "In fact, partnerships formed by friends probably have a greater risk of failure because of the casual way in which they are so often structured and managed — relying on the strength of the friendship to deal with the challenging issues that inevitably arise in the life of any business. That doesn't mean partners can't be friends, but they do require extra care in due diligence, performance expectations, role descriptions, and drafting agreements."

"I guess the good news for me," Henry mused, "is that all my good friends in the industry are the same age as I am or even older, so I won't be tempted to invite any of them to be my successor!"

"That *is* reassuring," I concurred.

"What else do we have to think about today?" Henry asked, obviously pleased with his decisions so far.

"I think we should actually look a little deeper into your business for other opportunities to not only maximize value, but also to set things up so that, as you gradually withdraw, there is no letdown in momentum. In fact, ideally, the business would be on the steep accelerating part of another growth curve, like you described so well in one of our earlier meetings."

"What do you have in mind to make my business even better?"

"We talked about this to some extent back when we were discussing practice valuation. There are a number of factors that can make one practice worth more or less than another. In fact, in our formal valuation process, we consider at least 50 variables."

"Yes, I remember. Things like percentage of revenue that is recurring. Obviously, more recurring revenue reduces the riskiness of the business, which, in turn, should make it more valuable."

"Exactly!"

"But, because of the work we did together a few years ago, almost all of my revenue is already fee-based and generates a fairly even cash flow every month, so there doesn't seem to be much room for improvement there, if I do say so myself!"

"I'll certainly give you that one, Henry. You have been my model client for transitioning a practice from commissions to fee-based. In fact, much of what you have done to your business over the past few years has made it much more valuable — to you. What we need to be sure of now is that it becomes more valuable to your successor. That will not only result in a higher price for you, it will also appeal to a higher caliber of candidate.

"Perhaps the best way for us to approach this is to use the same list of factors that we consider when we are hired to do formal practice valuations, like the one we recently completed for you. Coincidently, I have a copy of that list in my briefcase right now. It is quite lengthy, so I am going to suggest that you take it away and evaluate your business on each factor the same way we do. Ask yourself if it should contribute to a higher or lower value than other, comparable-size practices.

"While some of the factors are quantitative and easy to assess, others are qualitative and take some subjective thought. Be totally honest with yourself in your assessment. This is not a 'pass or fail' exercise, but one designed to identify opportunities for proving the value of your business to a prospective buyer.

I already have my list for your practice completed from the valuation we did, so it will be interesting then to compare our perceptions once you have had a chance to do some self-analysis."

"Can I take a quick look at the list now?" Henry asked.

"For sure!" I handed Henry the document

Risk Factor		Premium	Neutral	Discount
Strategy & Potential				
1.	To what extent is the "goodwill" of the business dependent on the seller?			
2.	Does the business have a clearly defined strategy?			
3.	Is the business currently growing, declining, or stagnant?			
4.	Does the business have the capacity to expand?			
5.	Are there opportunities for additional income?			
6.	Is the business dependent on the seller's network & community presence?			
7.	Is the business dependent on the seller's technical expertise?			
8.	Is there a consistency of recurring income?			
9.	Is the pricing policy reasonable and consistent?			
10.	Are there diversified sources of revenue?			
11.	Does the firm have a competitive advantage in any area?			
12	How does the practice generally stand up against the competition?			
13.	Is the geographic location suitable?			
Clients				
14.	Is the profile of the client base attractive to the buyer?			
15.	Is the average age of clients attractive to the buyer?			
16.	Is the average tenure of clients acceptable?			
17.	Is the average account size reflective of the market?			
18.	Is there a high concentration of clients representing significant revenue?			
19.	Is client retention acceptable?			
20.	Has client satisfaction been formally measured? Score?			
21.	To what extent are clients already familiar with the buyer?			

Risk Factor	Premium	Neutral	Discount
Marketing			
22. Is there a clearly defined market in which the firm operates?			
23. Does the practice have a unique niche or specialization?			
24. Is there a definable "brand" for the business?			
25. Is the advisor's personal brand larger than the business' brand?			
26. Are all marketing activities & materials consistent with the desired brand?			
27. Is there a replicable marketing plan to procure clients?			
28. Does the firm currently invest sufficiently in promotional activities?			
29. Are current promotional activities consistent with the target market?			
30. Has there been any negative publicity in the past?			
Philosophies & Processes			
31. Is the philosophy with respect to client service similar to the buyer's?			
32. Is there an effective client segmentation regime in place?			
33. Is the investment philosophy compatible with the buyer's?			
34. Is the financial planning philosophy compatible with the buyer's?			
35. Are the planning & investment processes compatible with the buyer's?			
36. Is there a high concentration of holdings in client portfolios?			
Staffing & Systems			
37. Are systems and technology up to date?			
38. Are policies and processes documented?			
39. Are client records accurate and complete?			
40. Is support staff tenure and turnover acceptable?			
41. Is the business dependent on key personnel?			
42. Do all team members have the required credentials & experience?			
43. How well do team members know the buyer?			
44. How likely are team members to stay with the buyer?			
45. Is the business dependent on outside resources?			

Risk Factor	Premium	Neutral	Discount
Structure & Legal			
46. Does the seller have ability to transfer the business without restriction?			
47. Are all current shareholders in agreement with sale of the business?			
48. Does the buyer have the ability to purchase the majority/ full stake?			
49. Is there protection of minority interest rights?			
50. Is the buyer acquiring a "Book of business" or a "Business"?			
51. Will the current dealer firm/sponsor assist with financing the purchase?			
52. Are proposed deal terms favorable to the buyer or the seller?			
53. Have there been any compliance or legal issues in the past?			
54. Are there any outstanding compliance or legal issues?			

"The process is simple — after you have thought through each question, put a check mark in the appropriate column. If you feel the answer works in favor of a higher price, check the 'Premium' column. If it negatively affects value, check the 'Discount' column, and if, in your view, it should have no impact on the price, check the 'Neutral' column.

When we do this as part of a practice valuation, we then add up the columns to get an overall perspective on a practice. It is important to note, however, that there is no magic formula that says if you score this many in one column, it automatically warrants a higher or lower price. That said, if most of the check marks are in the Premium column, we are probably looking at a practice that is above average; most in the Discount column suggests below average, and so on. While certainly not the only or final determination, we use this assessment to help inform our valuation.

"I am sure you do something similar when you first consider the situation of a potential new client."

"You are absolutely right," Henry conceded. "My informal process is to sit by myself for 10–15 minutes after meeting with a prospective client to try to visualize what it would be like to work with them. What are the positives and negatives? Are they realistic in their expectations? Will they be high or low maintenance? Does the situation warrant the work I am expected to do? And so on. I'm not trying to eliminate anyone so much as I am trying to ensure we are good fit."

"Precisely!" I agreed. "And when we do this exercise as part of a formal valuation, we are not looking to expose all the faults that might reduce the price but, rather, for the places where a buyer can gain leverage. That's why we don't 'score' the numbers, so to speak. What one person considers a deficiency, someone else might see as an opportunity.

"For example, one of the questions asks if there is a concentration of products. Some potential buyers might worry if there is, while others would see it as opening the door to offering additional products and services."

Henry was eyeing the list. "I can see quite a few places where I'll be ticking the 'premium' box," he said.

"I'm sure I'll agree with you on most, if not all of them," I suggested.

"There are a couple of other benefits to this exercise. First, it will help you put your 'story' together about what a great practice you have when you are talking to prospective successors. Second, it will give you clarity around the type of person to whom you want to transition your business. If you've made your practice into the best it could be by the time you start your exit plan, you will have some very specific ideas about the qualifications and character of the person to whom you are going to bequeath your legacy."

"Yes," said Henry, "I can see that…" His voice trailed off as he was thinking hard about something — or someone.

I took that as a sign we should probably take a break in our discussions, so I suggested a refill of our coffee cups. Henry said he would be along shortly.

When I returned to the boardroom, it was obvious that Henry had never left his chair. I could also see that he had gone ahead and checked off a few of the questions — all in the "Premium" column. I made him put it down.

"I think it is best, Henry, if you take some time to complete that checklist. If it is going to be of value to you, you have to be as objective as you can be. Try to put yourself in the shoes of a potential successor and ask yourself, 'Would I buy my business? If so, why? If so, how much would I pay? Why wouldn't I pay more?' And so on. A bit of time reflecting will go a long way."

"Yeah, I'll do that," Henry agreed as he put the list aside, but not completely out of view. "I was just checking off the obvious ones!"

I relented, "It appears to me that we're not going to get much else accomplished today until we look more carefully at that list, are we?"

"I admit, I am intrigued by the questions," Henry said, "and somewhat anxious to see how I score, so to speak."

"Okay, here's what we'll do to feed your interest a bit. Let's take a couple of what I believe to be the most important and relevant questions in your case and talk about them together. That will give you some idea of the sort of reasoning we use in valuing a practice. Then will you agree to take the list away and complete it thoughtfully?"

"Deal!" Henry declared with tempered excitement. "Which questions do you want to look at?"

"Remember that the purpose of these questions is to identify opportunities for you to position the business so your 'heir to the throne' sees it in the best light possible. With that in mind, there are a couple of key areas where you currently have a large personal influence that might have a considerable impact on the success of the transition. If we can properly manage these things between now and your exit date, we will go a long way to maximizing value."

"Let's go," Henry prodded. "What's first?"

"Goodwill," I responded. "It's actually the first question on the list."

"Oh, there's lots of goodwill in the business," Henry reacted immediately. "Clients love us, we have a good reputation in the community, and other professionals respect us. I'd certainly check goodwill off in the 'premium price' column."

"I would too — if we were only talking about your 'personal' goodwill. However, a potential buyer is going to be more interested in the 'corporate' goodwill of your business. I suspect that much of the 'love, reputation, and respect' you just described is directed at you, rather than your business."

"I'd argue they are one and the same," Henry countered.

"And I would agree with that. In fact, that is exactly the issue. If they are one and the same, what happens to that goodwill when you walk out the door?"

"It goes with me?" Henry supposed, somewhat sheepishly.

"Most of it anyway, unless something is done to prevent that," I suggested.

"Of course, there is obviously some spill-over, and there are certain aspects of your business where, in fact, the corporate goodwill is probably greater than your personal goodwill. For example, I know from our previous work together that clients now go directly to your support staff with administration items. They would probably be surprised if you tried to help them with some of their service requests!"

"That was the plan, wasn't it, Coach?" Henry teased.

"Yes, it was, and congrats on getting to where your clients feel so comfortable dealing directly with your support team on administrative matters. But, obviously, there are aspects of your business where 'you're the man' and the only person clients want to talk to."

"For sure — anything related to markets, portfolio design, insurance programs, or financial plans — my role as their advisor."

"And when you retire, to whom will they turn?"

"My successor, of course!" Henry reacted, as if it were a really dumb question.

"And to what extent will they know and trust your successor, compared to you?"

The answer was so obvious that Henry didn't even answer.

"You've spent 25 years building your credibility, your reputation, and relationships — with clients, with centers of influence, with lawyers, accountants, and bankers, with suppliers, with Head Office staff, and with the community. You are the business. The business is you. Your personal goodwill has underpinned your success.

"What we have to ensure is that as much of your personal goodwill as possible is transferred to your firm's corporate goodwill before you exit the business. In that way, your successor inherits the benefits of your life of building a great reputation. In exchange, you gain confidence in the probability of them realizing the full potential of the business. That means greater financial security to you and better peace of mind regarding your legacy. Does that make sense?"

"Regrettably, yes," Henry conceded.

"So," I suggested, "maybe the goodwill question gets a check mark in the discount column — for now? That's not because it is a bad thing. After all, as we said, you are the guy who built the business, so naturally, most of the goodwill rests with you. However, this alerts us to the fact that we have some work to do in order to leverage some of your personal goodwill into goodwill for the firm overall."

"And how do we do that?" Henry asked.

"There are a number of specific things we can do right away, but bear in mind that you built your reputation over 25 years, so we can't expect to transfer all your personal goodwill to the firm overnight. That said, the basic approach is to position the others in your practice in place of you.

"First of all, make sure your clients and centers of influence know who everyone in your office is and what they do. Personally introduce them whenever possible. You can even give people titles that elevate their stature; for example, your Office Manager can become Vice-President, Service Excellence, and your receptionist can become Manager, Client Experience, and so on.

"Take every opportunity to showcase others and refer to 'the team.' Have their names appear as the byline on articles in your newsletter. Instead of using the words 'I' or 'me' in your client communications, use 'we' or 'us.' Feature photos of your team whenever possible. Share some personal stories about them.

"Let someone else on your team act as host or hostess at your client events. You will still be the face of the business, but it will become apparent over time that there is much more to the business than you.

"When you do have your successor on board, promote them and their expertise. Begin early on to let people know that the new person is a key part of your plan for the ongoing ability of your firm to serve them. Does that give you some ideas?"

"Sure does," Henry said, "and I think I'll enjoy promoting others. I have a great team, and they deserve more recognition. Things such as you have just described will do that, AND it will strengthen their loyalty to the practice. That has to add value for a purchaser!"

"It will, indeed," I agreed.

"What else?" Henry pressed.

"Let's go right to Question #2 — strategy. Unfortunately, too many advisors equate succession with 'slowing down,' so they begin to let their businesses slide at the very time they should be building them up. Which would command a higher price — a business that is growing or one that is declining?"

"Growing, obviously," Henry answered. "But what about the fact that some advisors, including me, *do* want less involvement in the business as they approach full retirement. Isn't that one of the perks of being an entrepreneur?"

"It is, so your question is a fair one.

"My counter, however, would be that the boss wanting to slow down shouldn't mean the business has to as well. You, in fact, are a great example of that with your plan to become a succession planning coach to your clients. If you can structure your business in a way that allows you to focus most of your time on that new role, you can work fewer hours and yet continue to grow your practice.

"You are a lucky one — you have the strategy already decided. Now all you need is a business plan that outlines the tactics to achieve that strategy   your marketing, sales, service, and resource plans. By the time you reach your transition date, your business will have positive momentum of its own that a prospective buyer will value and for which they will pay more.

"Does this all make sense?"

"Yes, it does. So do I get a check mark in the Premium column for Question #2?"

"You do indeed! Now take the questionnaire away and spend some time thoughtfully answering the rest of the questions. You can tell me what you determine when we get together again in a week or so. Okay?"

"Okay," Henry agreed, almost unconsciously. He was already looking at the questions again.

Another Illustrative Case in Point

Get It In Writing

Rachel was a rising star in the industry. After only five years in the business, she had built a substantial practice and seemed well on her way to a long and satisfying career.

However, having tasted the financial rewards of her work, Rachel became somewhat impatient for something even bigger. While she enjoyed her role as a solo advisor, she saw herself as the leader of a very large practice — and she did not want to wait even another five years to get there.

So when David, one of the leading advisors in her community, offered Rachel the chance to join him as a partner with the idea that she would take over the business completely when he retired in three years, she jumped at the opportunity. It would accelerate her growth plan significantly.

Things went along smoothly for the first six months. Because Rachel was so anxious to take on the opportunity, she had not asked very many questions about exactly what she was supposed to do with her time, so she simply busied herself with clients and learning the systems and processes of her new office. However, she did notice right away that David started spending less time in the office and that the staff was calling on her more and more to deal with administrative issues.

She was also a bit disappointed when her new "partner" did not seem to have as much time for her as she felt she needed. More often than not, he would say something like, "You are a smart person; you will figure it out." She also learned that he had made a number of decisions about the office without consulting or advising her in any way. It seemed an odd way, Rachel thought, for a partnership to work.

Somewhat frustrated, Rachel booked a meeting with David to discuss the specific details of the transition of equity and management to her. She was worried that they were approaching the one-year mark of a three-year plan and there was still considerable vagueness around how and when she would assume ownership and management responsibility.

Much to her shock, when she raised the timing issue in the meeting, David seemed surprised by her concern and said he hadn't meant that she would take over in *exactly* three years, but rather that they would use that as a working target date. In fact, he said, since her arrival, he was feeling he had more energy for the business and that, perhaps, he might stay on another three years.

Still smarting from that disappointment, Rachel asked about her equity participation. She was ready to start buying shares in the business according to the valuation they had discussed before she joined. Her thinking was that if she owned part of the business, she would be better able to influence decisions, including David's retirement date.

Again, Rachel was surprised and shocked by the response. "Oh, that was just an approximation back then," David said. "The business has grown over the past year, and it is a seller's market, so prices are going up. We'll have to come up with a better valuation."

Plagued by the change of plan and uncertainty, Rachel's enthusiasm for the opportunity fizzled quickly. Within another six months, she fully regretted her decision and resigned from the partnership to reactivate her former practice. Not only had she "wasted" a year and a half in her mind, she had grown distrustful of the idea of partnership. She was going to have to build her large practice on her own.

Coach's Recap

- To demonstrate your commitment to your succession plan, you should have:
  - A 'buy-in' plan that specifically details how your successor can acquire equity — timing, pricing model, terms, etc.
  - A development plan with milestones that dictates how, when, and what management responsibilities they will assume.
  - Defined job descriptions and performance measurements.
  - A compensation plan that rewards everyone according to their role and equity position.

- There is a distinction between transfer of *ownership* and transfer of *management*.
  - You can transfer partial ownership over time, as you intend to do, without giving up all management responsibilities, or vice versa.

- Having a detailed transition plan in place for the transition is important, even among the best of friends.
  - Partnerships formed by friends have a greater risk of failure because they often rely on the strength of the friendship to deal with the challenging issues that inevitably arise in the life of any business.
  - Partners can be friends, but they do require extra care in due diligence, performance expectations, role descriptions, and drafting agreements.

- There are key areas where you have considerable impact on the success of the transition. If you properly manage those things between now and your exit date, you will go a long way to maximizing value.

- Goodwill: You are the business. The business is you. Your personal goodwill has underpinned your success. You must ensure that as much of your personal goodwill as possible is transferred to your firm's corporate goodwill before you exit the business.

- Strategy: Too many advisors equate succession with "slowing down," so they begin to let their businesses slide at the very time they should be building them up to maximize value on transition.

My Succession Plan

Exercise #10 - Setting Myself Up for Success)

1. Evaluate your practice by indicating whether you feel each factor should have a positive (Premium), negative (Discount) or no (Neutral) impact on its value.

Risk Factor		Premium	Neutral	Discount
Strategy & Potential				
1.	To what extent is the "goodwill" of the business dependent on the seller?			
2.	Does the business have a clearly defined strategy?			
3.	Is the business currently growing, declining, or stagnant?			
4.	Does the business have the capacity to expand?			
5.	Are there opportunities for additional income?			
6.	Is the business dependent on the seller's network & community presence?			
7.	Is the business dependent on the seller's technical expertise?			
8.	Is there a consistency of recurring income?			
9.	Is the pricing policy reasonable and consistent?			
10.	Are there diversified sources of revenue?			
11.	Does the firm have a competitive advantage in any area?			
12	How does the practice generally stand up against the competition?			
13.	Is the geographic location suitable?			
Clients				
14.	Is the profile of the client base attractive to the buyer?			
15.	Is the average age of clients attractive to the buyer?			
16.	Is the average tenure of clients acceptable?			
17.	Is the average account size reflective of the market?			
18.	Is there a high concentration of clients representing significant revenue?			
19.	Is client retention acceptable?			
20.	Has client satisfaction been formally measured? Score?			
21.	To what extent are clients already familiar with the buyer?			

Risk Factor	Premium	Neutral	Discount
Marketing			
22. Is there a clearly defined market in which the firm operates?			
23. Does the practice have a unique niche or specialization?			
24. Is there a definable "brand" for the business?			
25. Is the advisor's personal brand larger than the business' brand?			
26. Are all marketing activities & materials consistent with the desired brand?			
27. Is there a replicable marketing plan to procure clients?			
28. Does the firm currently invest sufficiently in promotional activities?			
29. Are current promotional activities consistent with the target market?			
30 Has there been any negative publicity in the past?			
Philosophies & Processes			
31. Is the philosophy with respect to client service similar to the buyer's?			
32. Is there an effective client segmentation regime in place?			
33. Is the investment philosophy compatible with the buyer's?			
34. Is the financial planning philosophy compatible with the buyer's?			
35. Are the planning & investment processes compatible with the buyer's?			
36. Is there a high concentration of holdings in client portfolios?			
Staffing & Systems			
37. Are systems and technology up to date?			
38. Are policies and processes documented?			
39. Are client records accurate and complete?			
40. Is support staff tenure and turnover acceptable?			
41. Is the business dependent on key personnel?			
42. Do all team members have the required credentials & experience?			
43. How well do team members know the buyer?			
44. How likely are team members to stay with the buyer?			
45. Is the business dependent on outside resources?			
Risk Factor	Premium	Neutral	Discount

Structure & Legal			
46.	Does the seller have ability to transfer the business without restriction?			
47.	Are all current shareholders in agreement with sale of the business?			
48.	Does the buyer have the ability to purchase the majority/full stake?			
49.	Is there protection of minority interest rights?			
50.	Is the buyer acquiring a "Book of business" or a "Business"?			
51.	Will the current dealer firm/sponsor assist with financing the purchase?			
52.	Are proposed deal terms favorable to the buyer or the seller?			
53.	Have there been any compliance or legal issues in the past?			
54.	Are there any outstanding compliance or legal issues?			

2. Overall, I believe my practice warrants a price that is:

☐ Above average   ☐ Average   ☐ Below average

"You're off to great places! Today is your day!
Your mountain is waiting, so get on your way!"
Dr. Seuss

Chapter 11
How do I make it happen?

"I think you pretty much nailed it, Henry. What do you think?"

Henry and I had just gone through his self-evaluation of his business, using the questionnaire I had provided the last time we met.

"There is probably a little bias here and there," he admitted, "but overall I feel I was fair in my judgment of the pluses and minuses of my business. Obviously, I like the way it turned out with a lot more check marks in the Premium column than in the Discount one. There were only a few in the Neutral column, which reminded me of my first Branch Manager. He used to say, 'No one is a neutral influence around here. You are either a contributor or a detractor.'"

"Sounds like a wise man."

"He was, and I learned a lot about the importance of personal values from him that has served me well throughout my life and career."

"That is certainly evident to me as we have progressed through this whole succession planning exercise. You tend to put other people's interests ahead of your own — not in a totally altruistic way but because you feel if it is good for them, it will be good for you.

"All of which brings me to conclude that we are getting close to the end of this assignment. I think you are ready to put the finishing touches on your succession plan and begin its implementation."

"Really, it doesn't seem like we have been at it that long," Henry offered.

"I did tell you when we started that you'd find the process easier than you thought and a lot more fun — which also helped to make the time pass quickly!"

"Okay, so what's next?" Henry asked.

"Well, we can continue to plan all we want, but at some point, you are going to have to execute."

"Which means?"

"Recall when you were setting your 'earliest possible' and 'latest acceptable' dates, I said you needed to do that instead of circling a date on the calendar when you planned to walk out the door?"

"Yes, I really liked that approach because it gave me flexibility."

"Well, now I am going to ask you to do the opposite. I *want* you to pick the specific date on which you are going to pull the trigger on your transition plan. You already know *what* the plan is. I want you to tell me *when* you are going to get started. Next week? Next month? Six months from now? When are you going to take off the cloak of 'Henry the Planner' and put on the cloak of 'Henry the Implementer'?"

Henry thought for a moment. "What's wrong with today?" he asked.

"Absolutely nothing, as far as I can see," I said. "Remember the old saying — 'Today is the first day of the rest of your life.' So if the rest of your working life is about your transition to retirement, let's make it happen by starting now. Okay?"

"Okay!" Henry responded with conviction.

"So what is the first thing you are going to do to set your plan in motion?"

Again, Henry thought for a moment before saying, "Well, I guess I can't get started on my succession unless I have a successor. So the first order of business has to be finding the right person."

"Excellent," I agreed.

"We have talked extensively about what you want in your successor — someone in their late 30s or early 40s with at least ten years' experience in the business, who has demonstrated capability yet is willing to learn from you. I know you originally didn't think so, but is there anyone among your current associates whom you would now consider?"

"I have been giving this considerable thought and, unfortunately, I have to say that no one immediately jumps out as a great candidate. There are a number of good advisors in our office, whom I like as people, but I am not sure I want any of them as my partner for the next five to ten years.

"I have come to realize through this process that I can have the best ideas in the world about what I want my transition to look like, but if I don't have a successor who can really grab onto those ideas and work with me to make them happen, everything will be for naught. So I have to find the right person."

"Okay, so we have to expand the search outside your office."

"How do we do that — hang a 'For Sale' sign on the door?"

"I'm afraid that wouldn't do much for the confidence of your clients and staff," I answered. "But there are other ways in which you can let the right people know you are seeking someone special.

"You want to be discreet. As we have said so often, yours is a great practice, and a lot of advisors would jump at the chance to be part of your transition plan. They will tie you up with overtures and proposals.

"Some of your competitors might also twist the facts a bit to imply that you are on your way out of the business and, therefore, clients should be concerned."

"What about my team? Won't they be worried too?"

"They will be — unless you tell them right away what your plan is. Make it an important announcement of the launch of the next stage of growth of the business. Celebrate your new strategy! As we have said before, they are already wondering about your retirement plan. Give them confidence that they will continue to be part of a great practice and that their roles will become even more important."

"So how do you suggest I find the right candidate?" Henry asked.

"There are three approaches that I have seen other advisors use successfully.

"The first is to 'list' your practice, so to speak, with a 'broker' who specializes in matching sellers and buyers. Typically, they offer a website where advisors on either side of the deal can anonymously look at what is available to buy or sell. Identities are only revealed when two parties have enough information about each other to say they are definitely interested in meeting. Of course, non-disclosure agreements are part of the process at some point."

"But, as we have said, it is a seller's market right now. How hard will it be for them to find a buyer?" Henry asked.

"It won't be hard to find any buyer, but it will take some effort on their part to find the right buyer according to the requirements you provide. Once they do that, they will also likely become involved in putting the deal together. In fact, most of these 'matchmakers' earn a small percentage of the transaction amount as a fee for their services."

"Okay, what else?" Henry asked.

"The second approach is actually a different version of the first in that the 'broker' does not rely on an online meeting place but, instead, goes out into the market to proactively find advisors who might be interested in talking to each other. In your case, for example, they would do their own due diligence on your practice, create a profile of your ideal candidate, and then directly approach advisors they think might qualify.

"They should also perform some preliminary due diligence on prospective buyers so they don't waste your time with candidates who would not meet your requirements."

"How do they know someone might be interested?"

"Often they don't, so their job is to create interest. In fact, our experience is that we frequently find the best buyers and sellers among advisors who did not think they were 'in the market' at all because they are already running great practices. Once an opportunity is presented to them, however, they are often willing to take a close look at it."

"And these brokers are paid the same way — a percentage of the selling price?"

"Yes, they earn a 'success fee,' although some firms do charge a minimum fee to cover their work, regardless of whether a deal is actually completed."

"You said there were three approaches," Henry continued.

"Yes, the third method is to do it yourself. As you can guess, this requires you to do many of the things the brokers would do — create a profile of your ideal candidate, identify potential qualifiers, initiate a discussion, perform the due diligence, and put together a deal."

"That's a lot of work." Henry observed.

"It certainly can be; however, the advantage is that you fully control the process — the pace, the potential candidates, the due diligence, and the negotiation."

"I do like to be in control, but I am still not sure how I would go about finding suitable candidates," Henry said.

"Bearing in mind our comments about confidentiality, here is what I would suggest.

"First, make a list of qualifications for a good candidate, for example, experience, credentials, character, reputation, etc.

"Second, look outside your office but within your dealer firm for someone you know who appears qualified. They might be in the next town or on the other side of your city. I have also seen advisors move across the country for great opportunities such as you are offering, so do not rule anyone out who meets your qualifications just because they are not close by.

"You can also ask your dealer firm representative for the names of advisors they know to be interested in buying into another practice.

"Once you have a few names, you can approach them directly. Advisors within your firm certainly know who you are and what a great business you have. No one will refuse to take your call.

"If you would like to have more candidates from which to choose, consider telling a couple of carefully selected product representatives or wholesalers you know that you are open to taking on an associate as part of your succession plan. I say 'carefully selected' because you want to be sure you only have that conversation with people who appreciate the high quality of your practice and whom you trust to maintain the required confidentiality.

"These people are in a good position to help because they are in touch with a large number of advisors and are always hearing expressions of interest in buying into another practice, particularly in the current seller's market. Most would be more than willing to demonstrate their 'added value' by having an exploratory conversation with advisors they feel might be a good match on a 'non-disclosure' basis. Then, they could report back to you or arrange introductions, if appropriate.

"Does one of these approaches — the online matchmaker, the business broker or the 'do-it-yourself' approach — appeal to you more than the others?"

Henry considered my question for a long moment before answering, "I know I am going to be pretty picky about the person I want to work with for the next five years or more, so I think I'd like to be in control of the search process. I will try it alone first by doing as you suggest. If that doesn't yield the type of person I am seeking, I will revert to one of the other options. Does that make sense?"

"It does, and I am not surprised by your choice. You got to the level of success you enjoy today by having a clear picture of what you wanted and then working diligently to achieve it. As we have said, this is the next stage in the evolution of your business, so you should approach it in the same way."

"Yes, but in the past, I hired you to help me create my vision and keep me on track."

"And guess what?" I interrupted, "You did the same thing this time. Together, we have created your vision for transitioning your business, and I will keep watching and prodding you to make sure you execute. Fair enough?"

"Fair enough!" Henry declared.

"Okay then," I said with a slight hint of sarcasm, "the clock on your transition plan starts now — so get to work!"

———————————

Barely two weeks passed before Henry called and asked if we could meet. His voice on the telephone dripped with excitement, so I was anxious to hear what he had been doing since our last get-together.

"I know you have some good news," I started when we met a few days later in his boardroom. "What's up?"

"Well, the bottom line is that I think I may have found my successor," Henry said, trying to mask his enthusiasm.

"Wow, that was quick!" I reacted. "Tell me more."

"Well, I started to follow your advice to the letter. I made a list of qualifications and thought about the other advisors I know in my firm whom I might consider. That only added three people to my list, so I made an appointment with our National Sales Manager to see if he had anyone he would recommend I approach.

"When we met, I showed him my list of qualifications and described the plan in some detail — the five- to ten-year time horizon, the new client coaching service, and the gradual transfer of ownership and management. I told him about your valuation of the business and the type of deal I would need to make it all work for me financially.

"I identified the three people I already had on my list and asked him to comment on them as potential candidates. I then asked him if he knew of anyone else in the firm I should contact."

"I assume you are giving me all this detail because he was able to suggest the person who now has you so excited?" I guessed.

"Yes," Henry answered, "and it was him!"

"Your National Sales Manager wants to be your successor?"

"Yes, he does, and I was as surprised as you are, perhaps even more so because I know he has been doing a great job in that role. Everyone likes him."

"Tell me more."

"Jeremy used to be an advisor with our firm and, by all accounts, was building a great practice when Head Office offered him the job of National Sales Manager. As he said to me, the title and prestige attracted him, along with the opportunity to work with others on elevating their businesses. So he sold his practice to an associate in his office."

"And Jeremy doesn't enjoy the new role?"

"Actually, the opposite. He has been at it for two years and loves helping advisors with their business building and practice management. In fact, he loves it so much that he has begun to realize how much he misses doing it for himself. He wants to get back into the field and has been quietly looking for the right opportunity.

"And how close does he come to your profile of an ideal successor candidate?"

"Well, he has the experience of building a successful practice and selling it, so he knows what that is like."

"Right, but what about your other qualifications around personal values, philosophies regarding investments and insurance, attitude to client service, and so on? Does he have the credentials you want? Does he have the financial capacity to buy equity in your business?

"It sounds like he is a 'doer' who likes to make things happen. Will he have the patience to work with you for at least five years before he takes over completely?

"I believe you when you say he is a 'great guy,' but is that enough information on which to make such an important decision?"

"No, but I am pretty sure the rest will be okay."

I searched for another approach and said, "You know, my doctor told me recently that he figures half of the prescriptions for medications he writes for patients never get filled and that half of those that are filled are not followed through to completion. That means only one in four patients is getting the full benefit of his expertise and recommendations.

"Why am I telling you this? You have a plan and a process for finding your successor. I suggest you not short-circuit it. If it turns out that your National Sales Manager is the best candidate — great! But remember that everything we have done so far is designed to put you in control of your exit. Give yourself the best chance of success by having a number of people from whom you can choose. I am sure there will be no shortage of advisors who would love to be part of your plan.

"You are going to offer someone the opportunity of a lifetime to carry on the great business you have built. You have to believe that and treat the decision with the respect it commands."

Henry sat quietly for a moment. I wasn't sure if he was thinking or if I had simply let all the air out of his balloon by not immediately jumping up and down at the prospect of Jeremy taking over his business.

Finally, he said, "Of course, you are right. It is easy to get excited when someone who looks like the perfect candidate on the surface says they are interested. It's a bit like the prettiest girl in school asking you to take her to the prom. I guess I felt a bit flattered.

"But the truth is that I *am* offering someone a great chance and I do need to make sure I have the best available person because I am going to rely on them to make my transition from the business the highlight of my career it should be."

"So what are you going to do next?" I asked.

"Follow the plan," Henry answered. "I now have four names on my list, including Jeremy. I want to try to build that list to eight to ten candidates. Then I will do a preliminary comparison of each against the list of qualifications I made. If I am missing information, I will try to find it before I contact anyone.

"I would hope to narrow the list down to three or four primary candidates. I will either approach those people directly or ask someone else to speak to them on a 'no-name' basis, as I think that is appropriate. Perhaps you might be willing to do that."

"I would be happy to help," I said.

"By the end of that process, I suspect I will be down to only one or two candidates. Assuming we agree to proceed further, we will sign non-disclosure agreements and begin more comprehensive due diligence on each other. Even if there is only one candidate, I won't let them know they are the only horse in the race. I want them to work to convince me they are the right choice."

"I like your attitude!"

"Yeah, and thanks for reminding me that I am in charge of this process, which means I have a responsibility to make it work in the best possible way."

"You are welcome," I said. "May I also suggest you start assembling the rest of your transition team?"

"My transition team?"

"Yes. Anyone anticipating the transition of their business should have a team of specialists to assist them, typically a lawyer, accountant, tax planner, and financial advisor. So, before you get too far down the road, consult with the other professionals on your team on the wording of an agreement, corporate structure, terms of a deal, and the most advantageous tax treatment. Then, as you get deeper into discussions with your short list of candidates, you will be able to discuss what you want to happen more specifically. The good news for you is that, in many cases, the financial advisor quarterbacks the team, so you are ideally positioned to lead the process.

"Makes sense to me," Henry agreed. "I have great relationships with my lawyer and accountant, so I can put a team together quite quickly."

"Just a bit of caution here, Henry," I said. "Be sure that your current advisors have the specialized expertise you will need in this situation. If they haven't much experience in mergers and acquisitions of privately-held businesses, for example, you might want to consider asking them for a referral to someone who does."

"I can see the wisdom of that," he responded.

It was time to bring our conversation to its conclusion.

"So, Henry, it seems to me that we have done what we set out to accomplish. You now have a thoughtful, well-designed plan for your eventual transition from the business — at a time of your choosing and under the terms and conditions that you dictated. You have a disciplined process underway to find the right successor and a strategy for granting them ownership and management responsibilities.

"With your legacy assured, you can look forward to a proud and profitable exit from the business you have done such a great job of building. Thanks for allowing me to come along for the ride!"

"And thanks to you," Henry said, "for showing me that 'exit' is *not* a four letter word!"

Even as he spoke, I could see that familiar far-away look in Henry's eyes again. This time, however, that look was framed by a full-sized smile.

Another Illustrative Case in Point

Selling You as Successor

Eduardo had done many things right during his twenty years as an advisor to build his practice to a comfortable level. He had a diversified client base, a center-of-influence referral program that resulted in five to ten new clients each year, and a support team that literally ran his business. Five years previously, he had converted his business model to fee-based. Now almost 90% of his revenue flowed automatically each month.

As he approached his 60th birthday, "Eddie" began to think about his eventual exit from the business. He read everything he could on succession planning and attended any conference sessions devoted to the topic.

Of all the advice he heard, the thing that resonated with him the most was the notion that rather than "slowing down" in the last few years of his career, as many advisors did, he should "speed up," in order to maximize the value of his business before transitioning it to someone else.

However, Eddie did not want to work harder. Nor did he want to wait more than two to three years to increase his business significantly. The solution appeared to be to "growth through acquisition." By buying books of business and integrating them into his own practice, Eddy could leapfrog towards his retirement objective. The question was, how to find suitable books of business?

Eddie also knew that if he wanted to be a successful buyer in a "seller's market," he had to stand out as the buyer of choice. To do that, he needed to make himself "top of mind" when retiring advisors decided to sell their businesses. So he created an acquisition-marketing plan that included:

- Defining his "preferred practice," e.g. number of clients, revenue, AUM, etc.

- Crafting a marketing message to highlight his qualifications

- Developing a public relations plan to build his credibility and reputation

- Creating a standalone website that described his preferred practice type and client transition process, as well as the overall benefits to sellers in choosing him

- Advertising in industry journals and on-line "advisor match-making" services

- Demonstrating leadership within industry associations and his community to demonstrate the values that underpinned his reputation

In order to identify potential books for sale, Eddie told everyone within his firm — fellow advisors, management, staff, etc. — that he was looking to buy. He also directly approached a few of his competitors whom he admired.

He talked to wholesalers and other industry vendors because they typically knew hundreds of advisors and, as a result, they were often aware of plans to exit the business before they became public.

Eddie attended all his dealer firm's and advisors' association meetings and conferences, making it a point to talk to as many peers as possible about his acquisition intentions. He looked for "continuity agreement" situations — where he and another advisor agree to help each other continue doing business if one of them became unable to run their practice. He included a clause in the agreement that gave him "first right" to purchase the other practice if the owner died, became disabled, or wanted to retire.

Eddie also listed with companies that offered online matching services to financial advisory practice buyers and sellers.

By building a marketing plan that cut through the noise of the competition and having an active search program underway, Eddie identified several opportunities and was able to proceed into the negotiation and due-diligence phases of the acquisition while potentially competing buyers were still scurrying around trying to establish themselves as contenders.

Within 24 months, Eddie had acquired and integrated three books of business into his practice, resulting in an overall increase of 60% in AUM, revenue, and practice value.

Coach's Recap

- As you progress through your succession planning exercise, put other people's interests ahead of your own. If it is good for them, it will be good for you.

- Once you know what the plan is, pick the specific date *when* you are going to start executing it.

- You cannot execute your succession plan unless you have a successor, so the first order of business has to be finding the right person.

- Three approaches other advisors have successfully used to find their successors are:
  - List your practice with an online service that specializes in matching sellers and buyers.
  - Engage a broker who proactively looks for advisors who might be interested in talking to each other.
  - Do it yourself — create a profile of your ideal candidate, identify potential qualifiers, initiate a discussion, perform the due diligence, and put together a deal.

- To follow the DIY approach:
  - Make a list of qualifications for a good candidate, for example, experience, credentials, character, reputation, etc.
  - Look inside your office for someone who might be qualified.
  - Look outside your office but within your dealer firm for someone who appears qualified.
  - Ask your dealer firm representative for the names of advisors they know to be interested in buying into another practice.
  - Tell a few carefully selected product representatives or wholesalers that you are open to taking on an associate as part of your succession plan.

- Note that the best buyers and sellers often are not "in the market" at all because they feel they are already running great practices. When presented with a great opportunity, however, they may be willing to look at it.

- You have to believe that you are going to offer someone the opportunity of a lifetime to carry on the great business you have built. Treat the decision with the respect it commands.

- Give yourself the best chance of success by having a number of people from whom you can choose. If you have a good business, there will be no shortage of advisors wanting to be part of your plan.

- Put together a team of specialists, including a lawyer, accountant, and tax planner to assist with agreements, corporate structure, terms of a deal, and tax planning

- If your current professional advisors do not have experience in mergers and acquisitions of privately-held businesses, ask them for a referral to someone who does.

My Succession Plan

Exercise #11 – Making It Happen

1. **I will begin to implement my plan no later than** _____ (Date)

2. **Specifically, I will do the following in order:** (Choose 1 item per column)

#1 Action Item	#2 Action Item	#3 Action Item
☐ Identify successor	☐ Identify successor	☐ Identify successor
☐ Advise staff	☐ Advise staff	☐ Advise staff
☐ Advise clients	☐ Advise clients	☐ Advise clients
☐ Transition team	☐ Transition team	☐ Transition team
☐ Other (_____)	☐ Other (_____)	☐ Other (_____)
☐ Other (_____)	☐ Other (_____)	☐ Other (_____)

3. **If I do not have a chosen successor, I will:** (Check all that apply)

    ☐ Make a list of qualifications for a good candidate, for example, experience, credentials, character, reputation, etc.

    ☐ Look inside my office for someone who might be qualified

    ☐ Look outside my office, but within my dealer firm, for someone who appears qualified

    ☐ Ask my dealer firm representative for the names of advisors they know to be interested in buying into another practice

    ☐ Tell a few carefully selected product representatives or wholesalers that I am open to taking on an associate as part of my succession plan

    ☐ List my practice with an online service that specializes in matching sellers and buyers

    ☐ Engage a broker who proactively looks for advisors who might be interested in talking to each other

    ☐ Other (Specify) _____

    ☐ Other (Specify) _____

4. **My transition team will be comprised of:** (Indicate names, if known)

    ☐ Lawyer _____

    ☐ Accountant _____

    ☐ Other _____

Epilogue

Within six months of beginning his search, Henry had narrowed his hunt for a successor down to two candidates. His National Sales Manager, Jeremy, was not one of them. Through more specific conversation and deeper probing, Henry concluded that his time frame of five to ten years would be too long for Jeremy to wait to assume full ownership. It would not suit his "make-it-happen" approach to business and would inevitably lead to conflict between Jeremy and Henry.

Of the two remaining candidates, Kyle was relatively new in the business – less than four years. However, he had been highly recommended by an insurance wholesaler whose judgment Henry greatly respected. In their conversations, his enthusiasm, personality, and passion for sales were infectious. Henry really liked Kyle and felt he could drive the business forward.

The challenge was going to be financing a deal. Kyle did not have any substantial personal assets or a large bank account. Like most new advisors, he had drawn down on his savings to maintain his lifestyle as he built his new business.

The other candidate, Raymond, came closer to Henry's preferred profile. He had been in the business for eight years — three as an "articling advisor" to a large producer and five years on his own. Ray's practice was located about an hour's drive from Henry's office; however, his clients were geographically dispersed throughout the region, including into Henry's community.

By his nature, Ray was not likely to become a superstar advisor; however, he was building a solid business in a very methodical way. He believed in advisor education, which was leading him to accumulate additional certification and credentials whenever he could. He was well-organized and appeared to have good practice management skills that could be valuable as Henry shifted his focus to coaching his business-owner clients through their succession plans.

Not having a clear idea of which candidate he should choose, Henry sought my advice.

"It is too bad," he said, "that I can't somehow combine these two great guys into one. Then I would have a sales-focused, skilled manager to continue to grow the business in an organized but aggressive way while I did my thing with my business-owner clients."

"Obviously, you can't combine them physically," I said, "but what would stop you from bringing them both into your business to form a three-man management team?"

After a few moments of thought, Henry responded, "It would be more complicated, of course, but I think the synergy of energy, discipline, and experience could not be duplicated in one individual. Let's see if we can do it!"

Henry invited Kyle and Ray to lunch at his club and laid out the proposal. The immediate reaction was very positive. There were, of course, lots of questions around roles and responsibilities, compensation, ownership, and so on. All three agreed, however, that the opportunity was far too great to not find some way to make it work to the advantage of everyone. They scheduled further meetings to iron out the details.

Within six months, both of Henry's new partners were well ensconced in the business, and the momentum was beginning to build. Henry had begun his "business-owner client coaching program" with instant success. Four significant clients had signed up and were working through the process with Henry. Kyle brought new life to the insurance side of the business, and it was becoming a much larger contributor to revenue. The staff was responding well to Ray's management style.

At the end of the first year of the partnership, Henry's new partners each bought 5% of the equity of the firm based on the valuation we had done. Henry provided partial financing for Kyle's shares — something they calculated he would only have to do once.

Each year thereafter, Ray and Kyle would acquire another tranche of 5% based on an updated valuation so that, by Henry's "earliest possible date," they would own half of the firm. From that point, the three partners would devise a plan for Ray and Kyle to acquire the balance, depending on how close Henry felt he was to his "latest acceptable" date.

A well-designed plan, open-minded partners, and a sincere desire to treat all parties with respect assured that Henry's legacy would be even larger than his life.

Index

Symbols

80/20 rule 86, 95

A

advisor compensation 40, 47, 54
agreement of purchase and sale 16, 94

B

book of business 26, 27, 28, 31, 34, 35, 36, 41, 45, 54, 85, 91, 93, 94, 115
broker 167, 168, 169, 170, 177

D

discretionary cash flow 40, 41, 42, 47, 48
duality 106, 107

E

earliest possible date 69, 70, 80, 104, 182
emotional enthusiasm 24, 34, 51, 56, 58, 59, 64, 65, 66, 69, 101, 107, 111, 112
Every Family's Business 135

F

financial capacity 15, 24, 29, 34, 51, 56, 63, 120, 143, 172
financial/emotional matrix 58, 59, 64, 66, 72, 101, 111, 112
financial freedom 58, 59, 64, 65, 66, 69, 72, 80, 101, 102, 107, 111, 112
financial statements 43

G

goodwill 26, 34, 38, 150, 154, 155, 156, 160, 161

I

internal transition 88, 89, 90, 96, 116, 123, 125, 130

L

latest acceptable date 69, 80
legacy 2, 10, 12, 16, 20, 55, 90, 99, 115, 122, 129, 134, 140, 153, 155, 174, 183
lifestyle practice 25, 26, 29, 34, 36, 41, 48, 54, 63, 84, 85, 95

O

owner compensation 39, 40, 47, 54

P

practice growth curve 75

Q

qualitative 27, 28, 29, 37, 41, 42, 43, 46, 47, 48, 49, 149
quantitative 27, 28, 29, 37, 43, 46, 47, 49, 51, 149

R

recurring revenue 42, 48, 49, 148
risk factor questionnaire 150, 161
rolling ten-year trap 68, 80
rules-of-thumb 26, 27, 31, 35, 38

S

saleable 12, 19
scalable 12, 19
seller's market 12, 85, 91, 159, 168, 169, 175
Stephen Covey 101, 129
strategy 11, 18, 24, 26, 27, 44, 49, 55, 74, 81, 91, 106, 107, 110, 111, 150, 156, 157, 161, 167, 174, 186
Strategy 150, 160, 161

T

terrible toos 2, 11
"They will be — unless you tell them right away what your plan is. Make it an 167
Tom Deans 135
transition team 173, 179

V

valuation 15, 26, 27, 28, 31, 32, 36, 37, 38, 39, 40, 41, 42, 43, 44, 45, 46, 47, 48, 51, 73, 78, 79, 86, 90, 96, 103, 116, 126, 139, 148, 149, 152, 153, 159, 171, 182, 186

Recommended Reading

(In alphabetic order)

50 Hurdles — Business Transition Simplified
Ian R. Campbell with H. Christopher Nobes — www.50hurdles.com

Built to Sell — Turn Your Business into One You Can Sell
John Warrillow, Flip Jet Media — www.builttosell.com

Buy-Sell Agreements — For Closely Held and Family Businesses
Z. Christopher Mercer, Peabody Press — www.mercercapital.com

Dance in the End Zone — The Business Owner's Exit Planning Playbook
Patrick A. Ungashick, Camarillo Press — www.navixconsultants.com

Every Family's Business – 12 Common Sense Questions to Protect Your Wealth
Tom Deans, Ph.D., Detente Financial Press — www.everyfamiliesbusiness.com

Exiting Your Business, Protecting Your Wealth
John M. Leonetti, Pinnacle Equity Solutions — www.pinnacleequitysolutions.com

Fast-Track Secrets for Making Your Business Saleable
Lorraine & Rob McGregor, Infinity Publishing — www.spiritwest.com

Finding Your New Owner: For Your Business, For Your Life
Jack Beauregard, STPI Press — www.theplatinumyears.com

Hire Your Buyer – A Philosophy of Value Creation
John Mill, Engagement Thinking Tools Co. — www.hireyourbuyer.com

How to Value, Buy, or Sell a Financial Advisory Practice
Mark Tibergien, Owen Dahl, Moss Adams, Bloomberg — www.wiley.com

Success and Succession — Unlocking Value, Power & Potential
Eric Hehman, Jay Hummel, Tim Kochis, Wiley — www.wiley.com

Succession Planning for Financial Advisors — Building an Enduring Business
David Grau Sr. FP Transitions, Wiley — www.wiley.com

The $10 Trillion Opportunity — A Guide for Professional Advisors
Richard E. Jackim, Perry Phillips, EPI — www.exit-planning-institute.org

About George Hartman

George Hartman began his 40-year career in financial services as an insurance advisor before entering his company's Head Office to take on various roles including Director of Training, Manager of Advanced Marketing, and Regional Vice President.

In 1985, George joined an investment management firm where, under his direction as Vice-President, Marketing, the assets of that firm grew from $70 million to more than $600 million in six years.

George is an insightful industry observer and prolific writer. In 1992, he published one of the first authoritative books for consumers and their advisors on asset allocation — *Risk is a Four Letter Word*, which immediately became a best seller, as did the 2001 sequel, *Risk is STILL a Four Letter Word*. His third book, *Blunder, Wonder, Thunder — Powering Your Practice to New Heights* placed #1 on the Globe & Mail's Business Book Best-Seller list in its first week of release.

For more than 10 years, George has written a monthly column *The Coach's Forum* for the Canadian trade journal *Investment Executive* and is a regular guest on *Building Your Business* television broadcast on IE:TV.

George has been a featured speaker at numerous conferences in Canada, the US, Mexico, Germany, the Caribbean, Japan, Singapore, Malaysia and New Zealand, including the prestigious Million Dollar Round Table (MDRT) and Top of the Table annual meetings. As one of the industry's leading advisor strategists, practice management mentors and practice valuation experts, he coaches top-producing advisors in Canada and the US and consults with financial services firms on their business strategy and succession plans.

George is President & CEO of Market Logics Inc. an organization dedicated to helping advisors and financial services firms realize the true potential of their business. He has a Master's Degree in Business Administration (MBA) from Wilfrid Laurier University. He sits on the board of directors of PlanPlus Inc., a global wealth management software developer, as well as several other private companies.

George lives in Toronto, Ontario, Canada with his wife, Julie, their son, Jack and Charlie, the dog.

For information regarding our coaching and consulting programs, or to enquire about George's availability to speak at your conference, please email: info@marketlogics.ca.

Speaking, Coaching & Consulting

Speaking

George Hartman's engaging style, humor and industry-specific knowledge have made him highly sought after as a keynote speaker, workshop facilitator, webcast host and training session leader. With more than 25 years of experience delivering powerful presentations to audiences around the world, he has insight into what makes participants eager to learn and how to encourage their progress from "knowing" to "doing."

Having worked with hundreds of financial services organizations, George is able to craft content that is timely and imperative to the changing dynamics of the industry. Topic areas have included:

- Marketing and business development
- Productivity and profitability
- Practice management "best practices"
- Succession and transition planning
- Valuation and maximizing practice value
- …and many more

George collaborates with each presentation sponsor to identify key messaging, relevance to the audience and the organization, fit within the context of current conditions and the knowledge or change of behavior desired. Participants become informed, invigorated, and involved!

Coaching

Financial advisors define success in their own way. For some, it means building a huge practice — with many clients and a large support team. Others want a simpler model, with fewer clients in a narrow market. Some are concerned about work/life balance or their eventual transition out of the business.

Market Logics' highly disciplined approach evaluates an advisor's objectives against the most successful practices in the industry. We, then, custom design an Action Plan to create a unique and personalized roadmap to success. Ongoing coaching ensures adherence to the plan and continuous improvement to reflect actual experience against objectives.

Our coaching programs include:
- *Powering Your Practice*™
- *Succeeding at Succession*™
- Custom design around specific needs

Consulting

The financial services industry is dynamic and increasingly complex. Many organizations, because of retirement, downsizing, or other trends, are finding themselves short on management talent who have broad-based and relevant experience in areas that are critical to the ongoing viability of their business.

Market Logics provides the opportunity to engage fully qualified, long-term industry professionals for specific projects, without having to search for these talented people, hire and on-board them into the organization, manage their activities or deal with employer/employee issues.

For each assignment, Market Logics draws from our extensive network of specifically qualified individuals, assembles them into a highly efficient and effective team, and coordinates their activities and output. This ensures our clients receive the best advice, performance, and effort for the lowest cost.

Specific areas of expertise include:
- Strategic planning
- Market research
- Marketing communications
- Driving sales
- Training program audits
- Training program development
- Internal succession planning
- …and many more

For information regarding our coaching and consulting programs, or to enquire about George's availability to speak at your conference, please contact Julie Bredin at 416.489.4848; by email at info@marketlogics.ca, or visit our website www.marketlogics.ca.

Notes

Notes

Notes

Notes

Notes

Notes

EXIT
IS NOT A FOUR
LETTER
WORD

HOW TO TRANSITION YOUR PRACTICE
PROFITABLY AND PROUDLY

ORDER more copies of EXIT is NOT a Four Letter Word

"A Gift that says your Legacy is Important"

Fax completed form to 416.849.0083 or
email info@marketlogics.ca

NAME: _____

ADDRESS: _____

CITY: _____ STATE/PROVINCE: _____ ZIP/POSTAL CODE: _____

PHONE: _____ EMAIL: _____

SHIP TO ADDRESS BELOW (IF DIFFERENT FROM ABOVE)

NAME: _____

ADDRESS: _____

CITY: _____ STATE/PROVINCE: _____ ZIP/POSTAL CODE: _____

PHONE: _____ EMAIL: _____

*Plus applicable taxes & shipping. Books ship same day orders are
received and typically arrive within 3 to 5 business days.

CREDIT CARD: ☐ VISA   ☐ MASTERCARD   ☐ AMERICAN EXPRESS

CREDIT CARD #: _____

EXPIRY DATE: _____

NAME ON CARD: _____

EXIT
IS NOT A FOUR
LETTER
WORD

**HOW TO TRANSITION YOUR PRACTICE
PROFITABLY AND PROUDLY**

ORDER more copies of EXIT is NOT a Four Letter Word
"A Gift that says your Legacy is Important"

Fax completed form to 416.849.0083 or
email info@marketlogics.ca

NAME: _____

ADDRESS: _____

CITY: _____ STATE/PROVINCE: _____ ZIP/POSTAL CODE: _____

PHONE: _____ EMAIL: _____

SHIP TO ADDRESS BELOW (IF DIFFERENT FROM ABOVE)

NAME: _____

ADDRESS: _____

CITY: _____ STATE/PROVINCE: _____ ZIP/POSTAL CODE: _____

PHONE: _____ EMAIL: _____

***Plus applicable taxes & shipping. Books ship same day orders are
received and typically arrive within 3 to 5 business days.**

CREDIT CARD: ☐ VISA   ☐ MASTERCARD   ☐ AMERICAN EXPRESS

CREDIT CARD #: _____

EXPIRY DATE: _____

NAME ON CARD: _____